"FASCINATING . . . a thought-provoking voyage into the minds of Americans."
—*Business Week*

"STARTLING . . . When I finished *The Day America Told the Truth*, I didn't know whether to shout about the revelations . . . or run for the hills and hide. . . . Exposes for us things about ourselves that I've never met in any surveys, or polls, or even seldom in private talk."
—Alex Haley, author of *Roots*

"GREAT AND CONTROVERSIAL FILMS ARE MADE FROM MATERIAL LIKE THIS."
—Alan Ladd, Jr.,
Chairman & CEO, Pathe Entertainment

"Plumbs the depths of our lyin', cheating hearts . . . should set alarm bells clanging in our national consciousness."
—*Boston Herald*

"STARTLING FINDINGS."
—*New York Daily News*

(For more raves, please turn the page)

JAMES PATTERSON, chairman of J. Walter Thompson, is one of advertising's most respected executives, as well as the author of six novels, including an Edgar Award–winner, *The Thomas Berryman Number*.
PETER KIM is a senior vice-president and director of Research Services and Consumer Behavior for J. Walter Thompson. Both live in New York City.

THE DAY AMERICA TOLD THE TRUTH

JAMES PATTERSON
AND
PETER KIM

A PLUME BOOK

PLUME
Published by the Penguin Group
Penguin Books USA Inc., 375 Hudson Street, New York, New York 10014, U.S.A.
Penguin Books Ltd, 27 Wrights Lane, London W8 5TZ, England
Penguin Books Australia Ltd, Ringwood, Victoria, Australia
Penguin Books Canada Ltd, 10 Alcorn Avenue, Toronto, Ontario, Canada M4V 3B2
Penguin Books (N.Z.) Ltd, 182-190 Wairau Road, Auckland 10, New Zealand

Penguin Books Ltd, Registered Offices: Harmondsworth, Middlesex, England

Published by Plume, an imprint of New American Library, a division of Penguin Books USA Inc.
This is an authorized reprint of a hardcover edition published by Prentice Hall Press, a division of
Simon & Schuster, Inc.

First Plume Printing, June, 1992
10 9 8 7 6 5 4 3 2 1

We wish to thank the following for permission to quote from previously copyrighted materials:
    The New York Times, for excerpts from news stories © 1990 by The New York Times Company;
    HarperCollins Publishers, for excerpts from I Never Called It Rape, by Robin Warshaw. © 1988 by
the Ms. Foundation for Education and Communication, Inc., and Sarah Lazin Books;
    Doubleday, for excerpts from Bill Moyers: A World of Ideas. © 1989 by Public Affairs Television, Inc.
    Business Week, for chart from the May 7, 1990 issue. © 1990 by McGraw-Hill, Inc.
    MCA-TV Ltd., for permission to quote from the film Do the Right Thing © 1989, Universal City
Studios, Inc. All rights reserved.
    Twentieth Century Fox Corporation, for an excerpt from the screenplay of The War of the Roses, by
Michael Leeson, based on the novel by Warren Adler. The War of the Roses © 1989 Twentieth Century
Fox Film Corporation. All rights reserved.

Ⓟ REGISTERED TRADEMARK—MARCA REGISTRADA

LIBRARY OF CONGRESS CATALOGING-IN-PUBLICATION DATA
Patterson, James, 1947-
    The day America told the truth : what people really believe about
everything that really matters / James Patterson and Peter Kim.
        p.   cm.
    ISBN 0-452-26808-7
    1. United States—Religion—Public opinion.   2. Public opinion—
United States.   I. Kim, Peter.   II. Title.
    BL2525.P37   1992
    303.3′8′0973—dc20   91-41621
                                                             CIP

Packaged by Rapid Transcript, a division of March Tenth, Inc.

Printed in the United States of America
Original hardcover design by Stanley S. Drate/Folio Graphics Co. Inc.

*For
Hae-Kyoung,
Bradford,
Justin, and my parents.*

For Mary Katherine.

We would like to acknowledge the invaluable contributions made to this book by the following people: Richard and Arthur Pine, David Hapgood, Barbara Groszewski, Laurellen Ridgeway, and the "eagles." And especially the fearless threesome at Prentice Hall Press: Linda Cunningham, Elizabeth Perle, and Marilyn Abraham.

CONTENTS

★ III ★

PRIVATE LIVES:
ETHICS, VALUES, AND DILEMMAS

★ IV ★

THE SEX LIVES
OF AMERICANS

★ V ★

MEN AND WOMEN
IN THE 1990s

★ VI ★

AMERICAN
VIOLENCE

★ VII ★

WORK

★ VIII ★

COMMUNITY
LIVES

★ IX ★
GOD AND
OTHER HEROES

★ X ★
AMERICA AND THE WORLD:
WHERE WE ARE NOW
AND WHERE WE'RE GOING

THE
DAY
AMERICA
TOLD
THE
TRUTH

INTRODUCTION:

What America Really Believes About Everything That Really Matters: Twenty-Three Major Revelations and How We Found Out

As we entered the 1990s, it became suddenly and urgently clear that a tumultuous change was occurring in America and the rest of the world around us. On every front—love, marriage, and the family; religion, politics, and the community; work, leisure, and our global position—the ground beneath our feet began shifting. Yesterday's verities had vanished. Unpredictability and chaos became the norm.

Here's what the average American was all about way back in 1950, compared to today:

THEN VS. NOW

	1950s	1990s
LOVE, MARRIAGE, FAMILY		
Percentage of women who were virgins at time of marriage	58%	35%
Percentage of adults divorced	2	9
Percentage of female heads of households	15	27
RELIGION, POLITICS, COMMUNITY		
Percentage who believe that religion is very important	75%	54%
Percentage who voted in last presidential election	63	50
Murder rate per 100,000	5.1	8.4
WORK, LEISURE, GLOBAL POSITION		
Percentage of women in labor force	31%	45%
Percentage of college graduates	6	19
Percentage of households with TV sets	9	98
Global manufacturing productivity rank	1st	7th

How do we know what we know about ourselves today? There is, of course, the U.S. Census, which is done every ten years. But how could we find out more about who we are and what we believe? We constructed a survey of our own, a very large national survey.

For one day in their lives, more than 2,000 Americans were given the opportunity to express what they believed about the things that really matter. Each of them answered over 1,800 questions.

The interviewing process was conducted during one week, simultaneously all across America. Fifty locations were chosen where the privacy and anonymity of the respondents could be guaranteed.

In addition, people answered a shorter version of this questionnaire. Thousands more cooperated in telephone interviews. This is the most massive in-depth survey of what Americans really believe that has ever been conducted.

How did we actually find out what Americans believe in their hearts? Why should they or we be believed?

It all started with this simple observation, a fact of research life: Most people *want* to tell someone what they really believe and what they *really* stand for. But that desire is tempered by the realistic fear that telling the truth will get them into trouble with their spouses, their bosses, their parents, their friends, or their neighbors. So, people rarely find anyone they trust enough to let all of their precious defenses down.

The most crucial technique we used in our testing is known as the cathartic process. We allowed people to unburden themselves with total anonymity. Once granted that, people were willing to truthfully answer questions of even the most intimate nature.

We guaranteed to the people we interviewed that no one who read their replies would know their identities—no one would know their names or addresses. In these circumstances, people felt that they could tell their secrets and share their true feelings. People told us again and again that this process was exhilarating. Men and women shared secrets and ideas that they had never before told anyone.

They could say whatever they wished—whatever they *really* believed. They had no reason to be hypocritical or to lie. They could unburden themselves and tell the truth.

Surprisingly, no national study had ever been done on what Americans really think and believe but, in order to compile our questionnaire, we analyzed thousands of studies on public morality conducted over the past thirty years for possible use in this study. Over 200,000 possible questions were considered. (See the Appendix for more on our interview methods.)

At the end of all of this research, we were surprised to discover that virtually nothing had ever been done to probe beneath the public position of Americans. No research had been completed on what Americans privately think and believe—on what we *really* believe, as opposed to what we think we're *supposed to* believe.

As a consequence, we herewith offer you an irresistible invitation to hear the truth from the following people:

Your wife, your husband, or your lover.
Your children.
Your mother and father.
Your neighbors.
Your best friends.
The people you work with every day.
The most powerful leaders in government, business, organized religion, law, and education.

One of the interesting results of the survey is that if you are like most Americans, no one knows what you really think or believe in. Not one person.

Nor do you know what anybody else believes. Chances are, you don't know what is in the heart of a single person, not even of those closest to you.

Just as important, the government doesn't know what the American people believe in or stand for.

Neither do our churches, our educators, or the press.

What you are about to read will change much of that for you.

Because for one day in their lives, we found a way to get thousands of Americans to tell the truth about what they really believe.

Below are some of the encapsulated results. The following twenty-three findings represent massive ground shifts in the American landscape:

TWENTY-THREE MAJOR REVELATIONS

1. In America, women are morally superior to men. This is true all across the country—everywhere, in every single region, on every moral issue tested. Both sexes say so emphatically.

Women lie less. Women are more responsible. Women are far more honest at work. Women can be trusted more. The implication, of course, is that women should be looked to for leadership in this country: in government, in both major political parties, in religion, in education, in business. Right now, very few women actually lead in America. (See Chapter 14).

2. At this time, America has no leaders and, especially, no moral leadership. Americans believe, across the board, that our current political, religious, and business leaders have failed us miserably and completely.

WOMEN AT THE TOP

Position	How Many Are Women
CEOs of Fortune 1000 Companies	3 out of 1,000
Member, U.S. Senate	2 out of 100
Member, U.S. House of Representatives	28 out of 435
University presidents	11%

Our void in leadership—moral and otherwise—has reached a critical stage. We still want leadership; we just can't seem to find it.

If America was a business, we would have been taken over long ago by the Japanese or Western Europeans. In effect, isn't that what's happened? (See Chapters 1, 21, 30, and 32.)

3. Americans are making up their own rules, their own laws. In effect, we're all making up our own moral codes. Only 13 percent of us believe in all of the Ten Commandments. Forty percent of us believe in five of the Ten Commandments. We choose which laws of God we believe in. There is absolutely no moral consensus in this country as there was in the 1950s, when all our institutions commanded more respect. Today, there is very little respect for the law—for any kind of law. (See Chapter 1.)

4. Young American males are our biggest national tragedy. Males between the ages of eighteen and twenty-five are the real cause of our crime problem. They are responsible for most child abuse. They are a violent, untrustworthy, and undependable group. At one time, our young men were disciplined in the military before entering the general population, but no more. (See Chapter 15.)

5. The official crime statistics in the United States are off by more than 600 percent. The recorded statistics are far too low. The amount of actual crime in this country is staggering. Sixty percent of all Americans have been victims of a major crime. Fifty-eight percent of those people have been victimized twice. (See Chapter 25.)

6. A men's revolution is bubbling below the surface of American society. It is coming as a strong reaction to the women's revolution. Many men now feel that women are using the cause of women's rights for selfish or frivolous reasons. (See Chapter 14.)

7. The 1990s will be marked by Moral Crusades. Many Americans ache to do the right thing but feel that there are no outlets through our current institutions. The first Moral Crusade is actually happening right now. Volunteerism is going to happen big time in this decade. (See Chapter 34.)

8. Americans now believe that the Japanese people are superior to us. Sixty percent of us believe that the next century will belong to the

Japanese. They believe that their children will work for Japan, Inc. The statistics and quotes will stun many Americans. The Japanese should find them even more compelling. (See Chapter 32.)

9. Lying has become an integral part of the American culture, a trait of the American character. We lie and don't even think about it. We lie for no reason. The writer Vance Bourjaily once said, "Like most men, I tell a hundred lies a day." That's about right. And the people we lie to most are those closest to us. (See Chapter 4.)

10. Community, the hometown as we have long cherished it, no longer exists. There are virtually no hometowns anymore. More important, there is no meaningful sense of community. Most Americans do not participate in any community action whatsoever. (See Chapter 24.)

11. One in seven Americans has been sexually abused as a child—and one in six Americans has been physically abused as a child. These numbers far exceed official statistics. The U.S. Department of Health and Human Services estimates that approximately 5.7 children per 1,000 in the population suffered from physical abuse and 2.5 children per 1,000 suffered from sexual abuse. However, these estimates are based on officially reported incidences of abuse—whereas our measures allowed us to tap into the vast number of children whose abuse went unreported. (See Chapter 16.)

12. The ideal of childhood is ended. A startling percentage of American children actually lose their virginity before the age of thirteen. They're losing their childhood, all of their innocence, in other ways as well. (See Chapter 13.)

13. Date rape is a second important and largely unreported epidemic. Twenty percent of the women we surveyed reported that they have been raped by their dates. Forty-two percent of Americans confess to having regular, violent sexual urges. (See Chapter 17.)

14. American workers and executives are now willing to make enormous personal sacrifices to be a part of winning companies. The majority of us want to be part of something bigger and better than ourselves. We want the companies we work for to be able to compete successfully. Americans have always wanted to be on winning teams. For the first time, many of us know that we're not. (See Chapter 21.)

Other significant findings in the chapters to come:

15. Homosexual fantasies are common in every section of the United States. One in five of us, both men and women, have homosexual fantasies. (See Chapter 10.)

16. We don't expect America to be number one in the next century, nor even for the rest of this decade. Americans, however, are still deeply patriotic. (See Chapter 31.)

17. The United States is far and away the most violent industrialized nation on the earth. (See Chapter 15.)

18. While we still marry, we have lost faith in the institution of marriage. A third of married men and women confessed to us that they've had at least one affair. Thirty percent aren't really sure that they still love their spouse. (See Chapter 12.)

19. There's a breakdown in filial piety. A majority of us will not take care of our parents in their old age. (See Chapter 24.)

20. Americans uniformly believe in the death penalty. One American in three would actually volunteer to pull the switch for an electric-chair execution. Ninety-five percent of us believe in capital punishment for some crimes. (See Chapter 25.)

21. The number one cause of our business decline is low ethics by executives. Who says so? Workers and the executives themselves. (See Chapter 21.)

22. Sixty-eight percent of us don't believe that America has a single hero right now. (See Chapter 30.)

23. A letdown in moral values is now considered the number one problem facing our country. Eighty percent of us believe that morals and ethics should be taught in our schools again. (See Chapter 31.)

I

AMERICA'S MORAL REGIONS

The Nine Moral Regions of America

Barely 125 years ago, regional diversity was so great in this country that it resulted in the Civil War, which left over 620,000 people dead—more than all other American war deaths *combined*. Today, with great advances in transportation and communications, America is a much smaller place. And yet our regional differences persist.

Our division of the United States into nine regions is inspired by Joel Garreau's landmark work, *The Nine Nations of North America*. Each of these regions has its own unique blend of culture, history, geography, and ways of life. We decided to see whether these regions also differed in terms of their moral "profiles."

Our research clearly shows that the people of these nine regions are remarkably different from each other in their moral beliefs and behavior.

In the following pages, we compare the moral beliefs and behavior of Americans from New England to the Pac (Pacific) Rim to Marlboro Country.

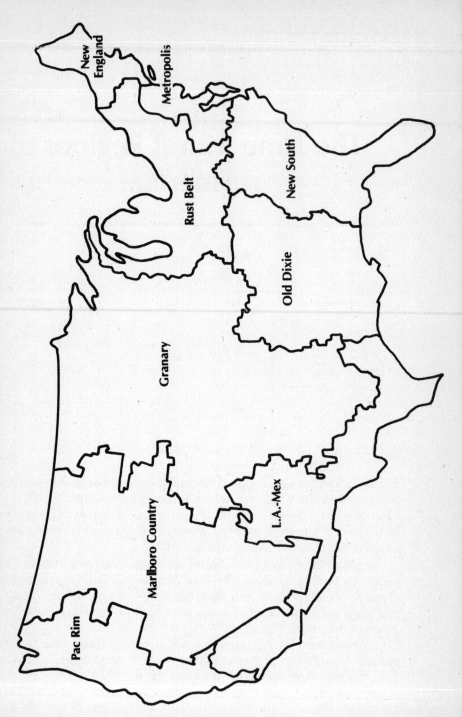

MORAL REGIONS OF AMERICA

New England

Metropolis

New South

Rust Belt

Old Dixie

Granary

Marlboro Country

L.A.-Mex

Pac Rim

MORAL REGIONS OF AMERICA

REGIONAL CULTURES OF AMERICA

	New England	Metropolis	New South	Old Dixie	Rust Belt	Granary	L.A.–Mex	Pac Rim	Marlboro Country
Population in millions	12	33	35	24	49	37	29	16	8
Percentage of U.S. population	5%	14%	14%	10%	20%	15%	12%	7%	3%
Geographic area	E. Connecticut Maine Massachusetts New Hampshire Rhode Island Vermont	N. Delaware N. Maryland New Jersey New York City W. Connecticut Philadelphia Washington, D.C.	Florida Georgia North Carolina South Carolina S. Virginia S. West Virginia S. Delaware S. Maryland	Alabama Arkansas E. Texas Kentucky Louisiana Mississippi S. Oklahoma Tennessee S. Missouri	Illinois Indiana Michigan Ohio W. New York W. Pennsylvania	E. Colorado E. New Mexico Iowa Kansas Minnesota Nebraska N. Missouri N.C. Texas N.E. Michigan South Dakota W. Wisconsin W.C. Illinois W.C. Oklahoma	S. Arizona S. California S. Colorado S. Texas W. New Mexico	N.W. California W. Oregon W. Washington	E. California Idaho Montana Nevada N. Arizona N.W. New Mexico Wyoming W. Colorado W. Oregon W. Washington Utah
Regional capital	Boston	New York City	Atlanta	Birmingham	Detroit	Kansas City	Los Angeles	Seattle	Denver

★ ───

PROFILE: NEW ENGLAND

Regional capital: Boston. Population: 12 million (5 percent of the U.S. population). Includes: Massachusetts, Maine, New Hampshire, Vermont, Rhode Island, and eastern Connecticut.

The Puritan birthplace of our nation, New England is the oldest region of the country. It is where many of America's great social and political movements began: the independence movement, which led to the founding of our Republic; the antislavery movement, which nearly tore it apart; and the temperance movement, which did much to institutionalize and legitimize moral hypocrisy.

Known mostly for moral probity and its great concentration of elite universities, New England has few raw materials, little agriculture, high taxes, and high fuel costs. It was the first part of the country to go into an economic decline when its mills and factories became obsolete early in this century. After a brief recovery in the late 1970s and early 1980s, it is once again in a period of relative decline.

Ale is the favorite alcoholic drink here. The region ranks second in drug use.

Compared to people of other regions, New Englanders rank *first* in the nation in:

- Giving to charity (tied with the New South)
- Cheating on their spouses
- Thinking that they're likely to be divorced in five years
- Spying on their neighbors

The people of New England rank *last* in:

- Being willing to kill for what they believe
- Believing that it's their moral responsibility to help the poor
- Number of drunk drivers
- Having violent sexual urges
- Carrying a weapon
- Discussing sex with their spouses or lovers
- Number of gays and lesbians
- Giving their best effort at work
- Number of unethical employees
- Job satisfaction

★ ——————————————————————————————————————

PROFILE: METROPOLIS

Regional capital: New York City. Population: 33 million (14 percent of the U.S. population). Includes: New York City and Washington, D.C., metropolitan areas; Philadelphia; New Jersey; and parts of Delaware and Maryland.

Metropolis represents the greatest concentration of wealth, status, and power in the country. On the other hand, it is also a highly polarized region with burned-out and abandoned inner cities that are the home for a large proportion of the nation's underclass.

Imported wine is the favorite alcoholic drink here. The region ranks fourth (tied with the Rust Belt) in drug use.

The people of Metropolis rank *first* in the nation in:

* Keeping their virginity till marriage
* Thinking about cheating on their spouses (tied with the Granary)
* Number of unethical employees
* Having confidence in the future of America

Metropolitans rank *last* in:

* Having ever considered killing another person

People here rank above the national average in:

* Being willing to kill for what they believe
* Giving to charity
* Having violent sexual urges
* Discussing sex with their spouses or lovers
* Cheating on their spouses
* Number of hardcore racists

★ ──

PROFILE: NEW SOUTH

Regional capital: Atlanta. Population: 35 million (14 percent of the U.S. population). Includes: Florida, Georgia, North Carolina, South Carolina, southern Virginia, southern West Virginia, southern Maryland, and southern Delaware.

It is called the New South because its fast economic growth, rising urbanization, and sense of its own future distinguish it from the rest of the South, which still tends to look to the past for its identity. The election of Jimmy Carter to the presidency in 1976 was a symbolic watershed for the New South and its emergence as a national force, as is Atlanta's hosting of the Summer Olympics in 1996.

Domestic wine is the favorite alcoholic drink here. The region ranks seventh in drug use.

The people of the New South rank *first* in the nation in:

• Giving to charity (tied with New England)

New Southerners rank *last* in:

• Spying on their neighbors

People here rank above the national average in:

• Having violent sexual urges
• Using force on other people
• Carrying a weapon
• Giving their total effort at work
• Being true to oneself and others
• Number of sociopaths
• Believing in "my country, right or wrong"

★ ───────────────────────────────────

PROFILE: OLD DIXIE

Regional capital: Birmingham. Population: 24 million (10 percent of the U.S. population). Includes: Alabama, Mississippi, Louisiana, Arkansas, Kentucky, Tennessee, southern Missouri, eastern Texas, and southern Oklahoma.

Dixie is an idea, a way of life—a way of thinking, acting, and living which, with one exception, has changed little in the past century. The exception, of course, is the civil rights movement of the 1950s and 1960s, which targeted Old Dixie and began to demolish the racial caste system.

Bourbon is the favorite alcoholic drink here. The region ranks last in drug use.

The people of Old Dixie rank *first* in the nation in:

- Being willing to die for what they believe (tied with Pac Rim)
- Believing in God
- Number of hardcore racists
- Believing that America still has heroes

Old Dixie people rank *last* in:

- Using drugs
- Using force on other people
- Number of sociopaths

People here rank above the national average in:

- Believing that it's their moral responsibility to help the poor
- Keeping their virginity till marriage
- Cheating on their spouses

★ ───

PROFILE: RUST BELT

Regional capital: Detroit. Population: 49 million (20 percent of the U.S. population). Includes: western Pennsylvania, western New York State, Ohio, Illinois, Indiana, and Michigan.

The traditional industrial center of the nation, the Rust Belt is now declining in investments, jobs, and population. Heavily blue collar and unionized, it is the biggest loser in America's transition to a post-industrial society. The Rust Belt is the region most associated with America's decline as a nation.

Draft beer is the favorite alcoholic drink here. The region ranks fourth (tied with Metropolis) in drug use.

The people of the Rust Belt rank *first* in the nation in:

- Believing in "my country, right or wrong"

Rust Belters rank *last* in:

- Supporting civil liberties (tied with the Granary)
- Believing that America still has heroes

People here rank above the national average in:

- Believing in God
- Number of drunk drivers
- Number of hardcore racists

★ ───

PROFILE: GRANARY

Regional capital: Kansas City. Population: 37 million (15 percent of the U.S. population). Includes: Minnesota, Iowa, Kansas, North Dakota, Nebraska, northern Missouri, western Wisconsin, northwestern Michigan, western and central Oklahoma, eastern New Mexico, eastern Colorado, western and central Illinois, and northern and central Texas.

The rural heartland of America, the Granary is conservative, hardworking, and religious. It is the "Field of Dreams" of America, the region most associated with America's idyllic agrarian past. As such, it is often depicted as the symbolic "real" America by filmmakers and advertisers. The Granary is often the last place in the country to accept social change. Indeed, an idea must "play in Peoria" before it can be fully accepted.
Rye is the favorite alcoholic drink here. The region ranks third in drug use.
The people of the Granary rank *first* in the nation in:

- Being willing to kill for what they believe
- Number of drunk drivers
- Thinking about cheating on their spouses (tied with Metropolis)
- Having violent sexual urges

Granary people rank *last* in:

- Supporting civil liberties (tied with the Rust Belt)

People here rank above the national average in:

- Being willing to die for what they believe
- Believing in God
- Giving to charity
- Using drugs
- Considering suicide
- Having ever considered killing another person
- Keeping their virginity till marriage
- Thinking that they're likely to be divorced in five years
- Giving their total effort at work
- Feeling job satisfaction

★ ───────────────────────────────────

PROFILE: L.A.–MEX

Regional capital: Los Angeles. Population: 29 million (12 percent of the U.S. population). Includes: southwestern and south central California, southern Arizona, western New Mexico, southern Texas, and southern Colorado.

L.A.–Mex is a culture divided against itself. At its base, it is a large Hispanic community. At its summit, it is an affluent, laid-back, lifestyle-oriented anglo culture which has turned conspicuous consumption into an American art form.

Tequila is the favorite alcoholic drink here. The region ranks sixth in drug use.

The people of L.A.–Mex rank *first* in the nation in:

- Being true to oneself and others

People here rank above the national average in:

- Believing in God
- Believing that it's their moral responsibility to help the poor
- Considering suicide
- Having ever considered killing another person
- Carrying a weapon
- Feeling job satisfaction
- Supporting civil liberties
- Having confidence in the future of America

★ ────────────────────────────

PROFILE: PAC RIM

Regional capital: Seattle. Population: 16 million (7 percent of the U.S. population). Includes: northwestern California, western Oregon, and western Washington.

We call this region on the Pacific Shore the Pac Rim because it is the region of the country best suited both economically as well as geographically to cope with and profit from the tremendous economic growth occurring across the Pacific.

A region noted for its natural beauty, it is the home of high-tech Silicon Valley. It is known for an almost religious worship of nature and a deep commitment to environmentalism.

Cognac is the favorite alcoholic drink here. The region ranks first in drug use.

The people of the Pac Rim rank *first* in the nation in:

- Being willing to die for what they believe (tied with Old Dixie)
- Using drugs
- Using force on other people (tied with Marlboro County)
- Discussing sex with their spouses or lovers
- Number of gays and lesbians
- Goofing off at work
- Number of sociopaths
- Considering suicide
- Supporting civil liberties

The people of the Pac Rim rank *last* in:

- Believing in God
- Giving to charity
- Being true to oneself and others
- Number of hardcore racists
- Believing in "my country, right or wrong"
- Keeping their virginity till marriage (tied with Marlboro Country)

★

PROFILE: MARLBORO COUNTRY

Regional capital: Denver. Population: 8 million (3 percent of the U.S. population). Includes: Wyoming, Nevada, Montana, Utah, Idaho, western Colorado, eastern California, northern Arizona, western Oregon, western Washington, and northwestern New Mexico.

Marlboro Country has the most land and the fewest residents of all of our regions. It is the "true west" of American mythical lore, the home of rugged individualism and hard, solitary living. Residents will sometimes drive 100 miles to see a movie.

Canadian whiskey is the favorite alcoholic drink here. The region ranks next to last in drug use.

The people of Marlboro Country rank *first* in the nation in:

- Believing that it's their moral responsibility to help the poor
- Having ever considered killing another person
- Using force on other people (tied with Pac Rim)
- Carrying a weapon
- Job satisfaction
- Giving their best effort at work

Marlboreans rank *last* in:

- Being willing to die for what they believe
- Considering suicide
- Keeping their virginity till marriage (tied with Pac Rim)
- Thinking about cheating on their spouses
- Cheating on their spouses
- Having confidence in the future of America
- Thinking that they're likely to be divorced in five years

People here rank above the national average in:

- Number of drunk drivers
- Discussing sex with their spouses or lovers
- Number of sociopaths

II

THE REAL MORAL AUTHORITY IN AMERICA

1

A New Moral Authority in America: You're It!

It's the wild, wild West all over again in America, but it's wilder and woollier this time. *You* are the law in this country. Who says so? *You* do, pardner.

In the 1950s and even in the early 1960s, there was something much closer to a moral consensus in America. It was mirrored in a parade of moralizing family TV programs: *Ozzie and Harriet, Father Knows Best, Donna Reed, Leave It to Beaver,* and even *Bonanza.*

There is absolutely no moral consensus at all in the 1990s.

Everyone is making up their own personal moral codes—their own Ten Commandments.

Here are ten extraordinary commandments for the 1990s. These are real commandments, the rules that many people actually live by. (The percentage of people who live by each commandment is included.)

1. I don't see the point in observing the Sabbath (77 percent).
2. I will steal from those who won't really miss it (74 percent).
3. I will lie when it suits me, so long as it doesn't cause any real damage (64 percent).

4. I will drink and drive if I feel that I can handle it. I know my limit (56 percent).

5. I will cheat on my spouse—after all, given the chance, he or she will do the same (53 percent).

6. I will procrastinate at work and do absolutely nothing about one full day in every five. It's standard operating procedure (50 percent).

7. I will use recreational drugs (41 percent).

8. I will cheat on my taxes—to a point (30 percent).

9. I will put my lover at risk of disease. I sleep around a bit, but who doesn't (31 percent)?

10. Technically, I may have committed date rape, but I know that she wanted it (20 percent have been date-raped).

Almost all of us have highly individualized moral menus like that today. We decide what's right and wrong. Most Americans have no respect for what the law says.

THE 1950s

In order to fully understand the decline of moral authority in the United States, it is useful to compare the America of the 1990s to the America of the 1950s. In the 1950s, America as a nation was at the zenith of its power. It had just won a World War, the result of which was to make the United States the most powerful and wealthiest nation in the history of the world.

The 1950s was a decade of optimism, belief in the future, belief in the nation. Conformity to external moral authority was central.

Political Conformity. Anyone who varied from the political orthodoxy of the time was defined as un-American. The House Un-American Activities Committee was one of the most powerful committees in Congress.

Conformity at Work. This was the age of the "organization man." The individualistic entrepreneur was replaced by this organization man, whose principal loyalty was to the corporation.

Conformity at Home. This was the age of the traditional husband-breadwinner family. The situation comedies of the 1950s showed nearly identical middle-class families with professional fathers and suburban, middle-class lifestyles. Most celebrated the supremacy of the American way of life.

Conformity in the Consumer Marketplace. It was the age of "keeping up with the Joneses." It was a time when the most common advertising selling theme was "If you're like most people . . ."

Indeed, belief in the American way was so strong in the 1950s that some social scientists began to speculate that a new civil religion of Americanism was emerging. Of this period, George Gallup and Jim Castelli wrote that there was emerging ". . . a shared public faith in the nation, a faith linked to people's everyday life through a set of beliefs, symbolized rituals that contained religious elements and overtones but were not formally associated with any particular religion."

A woman lawyer from Washington, D.C., said, "To be perfectly honest, some laws seem to apply to me, some I disregard. Some tenets of the Catholic Church add up, others are absurd, or even insulting. I don't need the Pope, the press, or some lowly cop to tell me how to live my life. That's the way I honestly see it, and I don't think I've ever actually verbalized the thought before."

As a consequence, Americans of the 1990s stand alone in a way unknown to any previous generation.

When we want to answer a question of right and wrong, we ask ourselves.

What we *don't* do is what people have done for a long, long time: take counsel and advice from our religious and political authorities, from the press, from our schools.

AMERICA IS VIRTUALLY LEADERLESS IN THE 1990s

Our leaders are still giving advice, but we are not listening. America's leadership no longer leads anyone.

We asked people to give letter grades of A to F to leaders in four categories: religion, politics, business, and education.

The highest grade that any kind of leader got was a C+ for religion. All of the others got low Cs or even a grade of D. C− was the combined grade average for leadership in America!

Why? One reason is because they have lied to us—over and over and over. Our leaders have told the most bold-faced lies.

So who are our moral leaders now? Well, the overwhelming majority of people (93 percent) said that they—and nobody else—determine what is and what isn't moral in their lives. They base their decisions on their own experience, even on their daily whims.

In addition, almost as large a majority confessed that they would violate the established rules of their religion (84 percent), or that they had actually violated a law because they thought that it was wrong in their view (81 percent).

We are the law unto ourselves.

We have made ourselves the authority over church and God.

We have made ourselves the clear authority over the government.

We have made ourselves the authority over laws and the police.

The fact is that whites are much more likely than others to follow their

A NATIONAL REPORT CARD: HOW WE GRADE OUR LEADERS

Institution	Grade	Institution	Grade
Religion	C+	Business	C−
Education	C	Politics	D

The Unprecedented Slide in Our Confidence in the Leadership Provided by Our National Institutions

Institution	Percentage Expressing Confidence		Percentage of Change
	1974	1989	
Organized religion	49%	22%	−55%
Financial institutions	42**	19	−55
Organized labor	18	9	−50
Education	49	30	−39
The press	26	17	−35
Executive branch	29*	20	−31
U.S. Congress	23*	17	−26
Major companies	31	24	−23
U.S. military	40	32	−20

*1973
**1977

personal sense of right and wrong. So are Jewish people and Catholics. The same goes for college graduates, liberals, and those earning $45,000 or more a year.

The people who rely most on religious or political authority (that is, laws) are blacks, Protestants, people who did not graduate from college, conservatives, and those who earn less than $10,000 a year.

There are important implications that follow from all of this. For example, most of us are not prepared—as so many others were in earlier generations—to sacrifice our lives for our country. Or for anything else, it seems.

When we asked what beliefs people would die for, the answer for almost half (48 percent) was "None."

Here is the measure of Americans' alienation from the traditional authority of God and country:

- Fewer than one in three (30 percent) would be willing to die for God and religion under any circumstances.
- Even fewer (24 percent) would die for their country.

LIES WE'VE BEEN TOLD BY THE VERY BEST

★ "I want you to know . . . that I have no intention whatever of ever walking away from the job that the American people elected me to do for the people of the United States."
—Former President Richard Nixon, during Watergate

★ "A little hyperbole never hurts. I call it truthful hyperbole. It's an innocent form of exaggeration."
—Donald Trump, businessman

"If anybody wants to put a tail on me, go ahead. They'd be very bored."
—Gary Hart, former presidential candidate

★ "One hundred percent apple juice."
—The Beech-Nut Nutrition Corporation. They eventually recanted as they pleaded guilty to over 200 felony counts for shipping jars of "100 percent apple juice" for babies (the main ingredient was beet sugar).

★ "I had little knowledge . . ."
"I've known what's going on there, as a matter of fact, for quite a long time, a matter of years. It was my idea."
—Former President Ronald Reagan, speaking on two separate occasions about his knowledge of Iran arms shipments

---

However, the baby boomers (people between the ages of twenty-six and forty-four) are more willing to die for what they believe (56 percent) than is any other group of Americans, including eighteen- to twenty-four-year-old children of the Reagan era (50 percent), middle-aged Americans between the ages of forty-five and sixty-four (49 percent), and those of us over the age of sixty-five (42 percent).

Men are more willing than women to die—or kill—for their beliefs. Liberals are more willing to kill than conservatives are. The young are more willing than older people are to die, and they are especially more willing to kill.

BY REGION: WHO'S REALLY WILLING TO DIE AND KILL FOR THEIR VALUES

(For a map of America's regions, see Part I.)

WILLING TO DIE (National Average: 52%)

Region	Percentage Willing to Die	Region	Percentage Willing to Die
Old Dixie	57%	L.A.–Mex	51%
Pac Rim	57	Metropolis	49
Granary	55	New England	47
New South	52	Marlboro Country	45
Rust Belt	52		

WILLING TO KILL (National Average: 35%)

Region	Percentage Willing to Kill	Region	Percentage Willing to Kill
Granary	42%	New South	33%
Pac Rim	41	Rust Belt	30
Metropolis	40	Marlboro Country	29
Old Dixie	34	New England	21
L.A.–Mex	34		

2

America's Number One Rationalization and Its Number One Result

---

"If everybody's doing it, why shouldn't I? If everybody is breaking the rules, am I a complete jerk to play by them myself?"

This rationalization has begun to take hold in all areas of our lives. Once woven into the fabric of our beliefs, it is where our most serious troubles begin. We no longer can tell right from wrong.

It also raises fear and doubt, which often lead to depression: Did I do the right thing? Does it matter anymore? Does anything matter?

Doubt comes with freedom as surely as ash follows fire. Americans in the 1990s have more of both freedom and doubt—and of depression too—than did any previous generation.

In interview after interview, we saw men and women grappling with the consequences of their new freedom to define their own moral codes:

- If no one I can trust is available to counsel me, how can I be sure that what I'm doing is right?
- Is the other person—my lover, my business partner—playing by some set of reasonable rules?
- What are the rules? My rules? Their rules? No rules at all?

Americans wrestle with these questions in what often amounts to a moral vacuum. The religious figures and scriptures that gave us rules for so many centuries, the political system that gave us our laws, all have lost their meaning in our moral imagination.

Most Americans (83 percent) now look back to their parents' day as a time when people were more likely to be moral and as a time when people clearly knew the difference between right and wrong.

In addition, we believe that our parents' generation was much more ethical than our own. We see most moral issues in shades of gray, not in black and white as our parents did. We've become wishy-washy as a nation. Some would say that we've lost our moral backbone.

"I FEEL STRONGLY EITHER WAY ABOUT THIS ISSUE"

We asked people if they see a set of current public issues as being morally "gray" or as clear cases of right and wrong:

Issue	Percentage Who See Gray	Percentage Who See Right and Wrong
Rights of criminals	57%	43%
Affirmative action	54	46
Teaching Creationism in schools	52	48
Premarital sex	52	48
The right to die	44	56
School busing	44	56
Homosexuality	43	57
Flag burning	38	62
Pornography	38	62
The death penalty	37	63
Homelessness	35	65
Fighting poverty	33	67
Alcohol abuse	33	67
Women in the clergy	31	69
Anti-Semitism	30	70
Divorce	29	71
Book banning	28	72
The drug problem	27	73
Prayer in schools	27	73
Birth control	27	73
Communism	26	74
Abortion	25	75

PERSONAL DOUBT

As to their private lives, half of adult Americans said that they had been in situations that caused them to seriously doubt the morality of something that they had done or were thinking about doing. We asked those people to tell us about the events that had caused those doubts.

Their answers give us a unique insight into what actually troubles the moral conscience of Americans, what falls in the gray area between the clearly right and the clearly wrong.

Did I Do the Right Thing? I'm Not Sure.

What follows is a sampling from our interviews that reveals the difficulty people have in deciding what's right and what's wrong.

- A businesswoman from the Southwest, in her twenties, married, recalled: "I had sex with a stranger. Very good sex, too. I changed my name to hide my real identity from him. I don't know what's really right or wrong in this age."
- A store manager from the Southwest, in her twenties, married: "Driving my car under the influence of drugs and alcohol. Also, sex with a stranger in a motel in St. Petersburg. I guess they were both wrong things to do. I'm not sure."
- A West Coast sales clerk, in his twenties: "Because of my religious beliefs, I'm supposed to believe that having sex with someone of the same sex is wrong. Yet I do it frequently. What's frequently? Almost every day of my life. The guilt is still there, though."
- It's the consequences of sex that severely troubled a teacher from the Midwest in her forties: "Advising my daughter to have an abortion led me into a long, suicidal siege. I'm not over it yet. I can picture a baby who never even existed."
- A woman from the Northwest, in her fifties, looked back to a time when she strayed during her first marriage: "My first husband was lazy and mentally abusive. I thought I was getting even when I strayed. I hurt myself more than him."

And many American men look back in doubt on what they did in war:

- "In Vietnam, I had very serious doubts if what I was doing was moral," said a West Coast post-office clerk, in his forties. "Right now, I have even worse doubts about it."
- A similar thought process took back a retired manager from the

Northeast almost 50 years: "I wonder about the bombing I did during World War II. The country said it had to be done. I'll go to my grave wondering if I'm a killer or not."

Some people broke the rules, or laws, for what at the time seemed a good reason—at least to them:

- A banker from the Southeast, recalled: "I forged my mom's signature when it was kind of important for me to do so. Otherwise, I went to jail."
- An administrator from the East Coast, in her twenties, wasn't bothered about cheating on a final exam: "I had a copy of the exam with the answers in hand when I took it. Does it matter? Do exams really matter?"
- "I lied to Social Services so I could feed my children, because their rules are unfair to white Americans," said a Southwestern mother, divorced and living alone.
- A vice-president of a service company in the East: "I rationalize stealing from my company because they have screwed me royally. They took thousands from me. I took thousands from them. Who's to say who's right or wrong? Not them, that's for sure."

Some told lies (or left truths untold) to protect others or themselves:

- "I lied about my husband being wanted by the law," said a churchgoing Northeastern woman.
- "I lied to the police and said I was driving, when my husband was arrested for DWI [driving while intoxicated]. He was the actual driver," said an office manager from the West Coast, in her twenties.
- A Northwestern woman who works as a store manager, in her early fifties, a regular churchgoer, said, "I eat out of loose foods, et cetera, around the store. I'll open packages, snack, then move on about my business."
- A truck driver admitted: "I was a hit-and-run driver. To this day, I don't know if the person I hit was badly hurt."

What's right? What's wrong? When you are making up your own rules, your own moral codes, it can make the world a confusing place. Most Americans are very confused about their personal morals right now.

III

PRIVATE LIVES: ETHICS, VALUES, AND DILEMMAS

3

The Private Lives of Most Americans

Kitty Dukakis, who actually kept her private hell a secret during her husband's presidential candidacy, said in a TV interview: "We are as sick as our secrets."

Most of us (55 percent) hide part of our lives from our closest friends. About the same percentage do things in the privacy of our homes that no one else knows about, that we would never tell anyone.

Here are some secrets that people had never told anyone before they told us in private interviews:

- "I've had three affairs during my marriage. I've never told a soul. There's no one I trust to tell."
- "When I was sixteen or seventeen, I used to rub my penis along my baby sister's vagina."
- "We're quite rich, but I steal from stores all around Beverly Hills. It's the most exciting thing in my life."

Americans hide. We hide, oh, how we hide ourselves—even from those closest to us.

We're not even honest with those we say we love. More than two-thirds of us would not confess a one-night stand to our spouses. Most people say that they've hidden their true feelings from a lover. The majority of us would not let our spouses or lovers question us if we were hooked up to a lie detector.

That's not our reputation, of course. In Europe and Asia, as well as at home, Americans are usually thought to be the most open of people—even foolishly so. Perhaps we're just good at pretending.

We say things that we don't mean (58 percent), we socialize with people whom we don't like (38 percent), and we don't stand up for what we really believe (42 percent).

So an awful lot of people (29 percent) say that they feel like a fake, phony, or hypocrite most of the time. That comes out to about 80 million phonies or hypocrites.

And that makes it a significant part of our culture—a national facade that hides who Americans really are.

The findings of this study contradict an age-old popular image. The truth is that Americans are reluctant to reveal who they really are—to anyone.

THE AMERICANS NOBODY KNOWS

One in four among us answered, "Nobody" to the question, "Who's for real?"

BY REGION: WHERE PEOPLE ARE TRUE TO THEMSELVES

(For a map of America's regions, see Part I.)

WHO'S FOR REAL? (National Average: 13%)

Region	Percentage of People Who Present Themselves to Others as They Really Are
L.A.–Mex	17%
New South	15
Rust Belt	14
New England	14
Marlboro Country	12
Metropolis	12
Old Dixie	11
Granary	10
Pac Rim	9

AMERICAN GENIUS AT DUPLICITY?

★ "The genius of you Americans is that you never make clear-cut stupid moves, only complicated stupid moves which make us wonder at the *possibility* that there may be something to them which we are missing."
—Gamal Abdel Nasser

★ ### SOME HONEST AMERICANS

It's not socially acceptable to say what we really feel and believe. Here, some people we interviewed speak their minds.

★
- "I've tried to like men, but I don't. They're pigs."
- "I don't feel comfortable around most blacks. A lot of them *are* niggers."
- "Here's what I like about women: good sex and good cooking."
- "I belong to an all-white club and I enjoy it."
- "I steal because they've stolen everything they have from us."
- "I'm a college graduate, successful, and I've never voted in a single election. The process is a complete farce."
- "I love fur coats, and I could care less about snarly little minks."
★
- "I don't have a single good friend left. Do you know why? Because I've told them all exactly what I think of them."

"How many people really know who you are—deep down, your true self?" One in five believe that their real self is known to just one person.

Nearly half the population honestly feel that nobody knows them.

There is no one particular person that most Americans think knows them completely.

Only 35 percent believe that their best friends know them.

Only 31 percent believe that their spouses know them.

We don't feel that our parents know us either, although more of us believe that our mothers know us (30 percent) than our fathers (19 percent).

We found distinctly different kinds of people when we compared the extremes: the Enigmas, who say that no one really knows them, and the Open Books, who say that four or more people know who they are.

The Open Books make far better citizens. They obey laws; they are active participants in the political process. Based on their responses, they are more moral people than the Enigmas.

Open Books let us read them because they like what's written there. Enigmas are much less satisfied with who they really are. They're twice as likely to believe that other people think badly of them. They're more given to violent impulses and more likely to act on those impulses.

Enigmas are more often men. Open Books are more frequently women.

If married, the Enigmas are more likely to stray both in fancy and in fact, and they are more than twice as likely as Open Books are to be divorced.

THOSE WHO KNOW US COMPLETELY

Person	Percentage Who Agree
Yourself	68%
Best friend	35
Spouse	31
Mother	30
Father	19
Lover	19
Sister	16
Child	15
Brother	14
Friend	11
Priest/minister/rabbi	5
Boss	5
Psychiatrist	4
Co-worker	4
Hairdresser/barber	3
Bartender	2

THE SECRETS WE KEEP

People to whom we *don't* confide our most private matters:

Person	Percentage Who Agree
Parent	48%
Spouse/lover	40
Child	36
Best friend	30

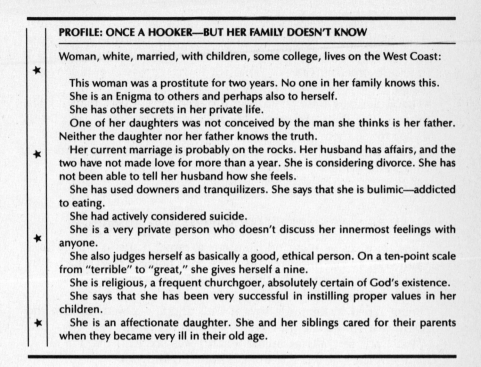

PROFILE: ONCE A HOOKER—BUT HER FAMILY DOESN'T KNOW

Woman, white, married, with children, some college, lives on the West Coast:

This woman was a prostitute for two years. No one in her family knows this.

She is an Enigma to others and perhaps also to herself.

She has other secrets in her private life.

One of her daughters was not conceived by the man she thinks is her father. Neither the daughter nor her father knows the truth.

Her current marriage is probably on the rocks. Her husband has affairs, and the two have not made love for more than a year. She is considering divorce. She has not been able to tell her husband how she feels.

She has used downers and tranquilizers. She says that she is bulimic—addicted to eating.

She had actively considered suicide.

She is a very private person who doesn't discuss her innermost feelings with anyone.

She also judges herself as basically a good, ethical person. On a ten-point scale from "terrible" to "great," she gives herself a nine.

She is religious, a frequent churchgoer, absolutely certain of God's existence.

She says that she has been very successful in instilling proper values in her children.

She is an affectionate daughter. She and her siblings cared for their parents when they became very ill in their old age.

SECRETS WE KEEP FROM OUR PARENTS

Our parents were obviously the first people from whom we hid our secrets. What are the most important things you never told your parents? What follows is a representative sampling:

- "That I'm gay," said a number of men and women who simply cannot be honest with either their mothers or fathers.
- "That I was a prostitute for two years," said a married woman from the Southwest, in her forties, who now has children of her own.
- "Became sexually active at age fourteen."—a housewife from the Midwest. "They'll never know."
- "That my relationship with my gay lover is a very dominant/submissive thing."—a market analyst from the West Coast, married.
- "Being sexually molested as a child."—a married woman in her twenties, from the Midwest.
- Fiscal secrets: "That I hate being poor. My salary for the past ten years stinks. That I'm really rather poor."—a college graduate from the East, in his twenties.

- Marriage failures: "How rough my first marriage was." "How my real relationship with my husband is." "That my husband and I were separated one time." "That I've cheated on my husband." "That I want a divorce right now." "That our marriage wasn't ever consummated."
- "That I actually hate them."—a divorced West Coast man, in his thirties. "My folks are despicable human beings, but I can't bring myself to tell them."
- "That I tried to kill myself this year."—a man from the Southwest who is still living at home.

SECRETS WE KEEP FROM OUR WIVES AND HUSBANDS

In time, most of us move on from our parents' home to a life of our own (although a large number of us move back home at least once). Now our most important secrets are those we keep from a spouse or lover:

- "Being raped by him. He says it's his right."—a woman from the Southwest, in her twenties, who lives with her lover.
- "That I was sexually assaulted when I was six years old. I'm afraid he might leave."—a single woman from the Midwest.
- "That I molested a girl when I was a little boy."—a man from the East, in his fifties, married.
- "She's really boring in bed. A turnip."—a retired man from the East Coast.
- "I screwed his best friend."—a supervisor in her forties from the West Coast, now divorced. "They're still best friends. Go out all the time. Supposedly share secrets."
- The highest percentage (71 percent) of secrets we keep are sexual in nature: "My before-marriage past." "Deep feeling about a previous lover." "The number of other lovers I've had. I had hundreds of lovers."
- "I am a cross-dresser."—a salesman from the Midwest in his forties, married with children.

The most tragic secrets may be our regrets:

- "Wondering if I should have given my ex-boyfriend one last chance."—an office manager in her twenties, from the West Coast.
- "I don't *like* him, never mind love him."—a married woman from the West, in her early fifties.

- "That I feel it is impossible for anyone to love me."—a single woman from the Midwest.
- "That she is the most important person I have ever had in my life."—a retired man from the South, about his wife of over fifty years. "I've never told her that."

SECRETS FROM OUR CHILDREN

Finally, we keep secrets from our children:

- "I get so scared when I think of their future. What we're creating for these kids."—a fitness trainer from the East, in her thirties, mother of two.
- "That I'm afraid of the dark and dentists."—a divorced woman from the East, in her fifties, mother of two.
- "That I often contemplate my own death."—a divorced woman from the East Coast with one child.
- "I was raped when I was seventeen. None of them knows."—a widowed mother from the Midwest.
- Other secrets are sexual in nature: "My life before marrying their mother. How wild I was when I was young." "That I was married

---

PROFILE: POSTCARDS FROM THE EDGE

Man, in his late thirties, white, two kids, household income about $300,000:

★ "Who am I *really*? Nice guy. Thoughtful. Remember my mother's birthday. Special surprises for my wife and kids. Love my kids more than I love myself. Try to do what I feel is right most of the time. . . .

"I've cheated on my taxes. I think it's wrong, but I honestly feel the IRS balances it all out. Everybody does it. . . .

"My folks' fortieth, I gave them a trip to Italy. I owed them even more. . . .

★ "Stole from department stores when I was a kid. Nothing big. Vandalized a cemetery once. Nut stuff. I don't know why. . . .

"No, I haven't had any affairs. . . . I feel a lot of violence inside me. Lately, there's been a lot of strong negative feelings toward women. Not anyone I know, just women in general. Violent images . . . strangling a woman in a bathtub. Like that. I'm not capable of it, but there it is. . . .

"Lying isn't one of my faults. I'll withhold sometimes, but I won't lie. . . .

★ "It's not our church that influences me, certainly not the government—at least, not positively. . . . My parents a bit. . . . More like this gestalt that I live by. God is a gestalt."

---

before. Pregnant when I got married." "That I'm not their real father."

- "I have not told them I'm running out of money."—a widow from the Southwest. "They will inherit nothing. They think I'm a rich woman."
- "That I really do love them but have a hard time showing and telling them."—a traffic manager from the East Coast.
- A technician, in her thirties, from the Northeast said that the most important secret she keeps from her two children is: "That they are the best things I ever had in my life. Why can't I tell them that? I just can't confide in my own children."

4

American Liars

How did we actually get the truth from people?

People being interviewed knew that their answers and stories were anonymous and safe. They could finally unburden themselves and say what they felt. For most people, it was exhilarating to be themselves for a change.

And this cathartic process was probably the only way we could have gotten at the truth around the country.

Americans lie. They lie more than we had ever thought possible before the study. But they told us the truth about how much they lie.

JUST ABOUT EVERYONE LIES—91 PERCENT OF US LIE REGULARLY.

The majority of us find it hard to get through a week without lying. One in five can't make it through a single day—and we're talking about conscious, premeditated lies. In fact, the way some people talk about trying to do without lies, you'd think that they were smokers trying to get through a day without a cigarette.

When we refrain from lying, it's less often because we think it's wrong (only 45 percent) than for a variety of other reasons, among them the fear of being caught (17 percent).

We lie to just about everyone, and the better we know someone, the likelier we are to have told them a serious lie.

Of course there are white lies and trivial fibs, and the lies we tell to spare someone's feelings.

Then there are serious falsehoods, and 36 percent of Americans confess to telling that kind of darker lie, which several people referred to as *real* lies.

We asked people to define what they meant by a serious lie. Their answers fell into four categories: Serious lies, they said, are those that hurt other people. Serious lies violate a trust. Serious lies involve crime or legal consequences. Serious lies are totally self-serving, are about who and what we are, masking the real truth.

Everyone lies, but some people lie much more than others.

WHO LIES THE MOST IN AMERICA?

- Men lie more than women.
- Young men lie more than older men.
- Gays and bisexuals lie more than heterosexuals.
- Blacks lie more than whites.
- Catholics lie a bit more than Protestants, and both lie more than Jews.
- Unemployed people lie more than those with jobs.

WHO TELLS THE MOST SERIOUS LIES* IN AMERICA?

- Men (40 percent) vs. women (31 percent)
- Homosexuals/bisexuals (52 percent) vs. heterosexuals (33 percent)
- Blacks (51 percent) vs. whites (33 percent)
- Catholics (36 percent) vs. Protestants (34 percent) vs. Jews (25 percent)
- Unemployed (42 percent) vs. employed (34 percent)
- Liberals (37 percent) vs. Conservatives (29 percent)
- Ages 18–24 (50 percent)
  Ages 25–44 (34 percent)
  Ages 45–64 (29 percent)
  Ages 65 and older (19 percent)
- People earning less than $10,000 annually (49 percent) vs. those making $45,000 or more (31 percent)

*Serious lies are lies that hurt people, violate a trust, have legal consequences, or are totally self-serving.

- The poor lie more than the rich.
- Liberals lie more than conservatives.

There is some good news about all this lying: Lying is something we outgrow. (Or truth is a privilege of age.) In any event, people lie less, in every age group, from eighteen to twenty-four on up through the decades. Those 65 and older lie less than half as much as those who are less than half their age.

WHAT IS THE ONE LIE YOU WOULD TAKE BACK IF YOU COULD?

- A construction worker from the East: "Telling this woman, nice girl, I loved her just to get what I wanted."
- A woman from the South who lives with her lover: "I told my mother I hated her—it was a lie."
- A secretary in her fifties from the Southeast: "That I didn't do it—in school—with a teacher, when really I did."
- A man in his thirties from the East Coast, bisexual, married: "Telling my mother I'm not a transvestite."
- "That my husband is not the father of our first child."—a woman from the East Coast, in her forties.
- "How many men I had sex with before we met. There were a good dozen. And maybe a not-so-good dozen."—a woman from the East, who said that she has been faithful to her husband during their marriage.
- "I had a social disease and, later, she found out anyway."—a retired man from the East, who reported four affairs during his marriage.

THE POWER OF A LIE

★ "Lying is a way of gaining power over other people through manipulating them in various ways. This is something that children learn. They also learn to keep secrets. Sometimes secrets are deceptive, and sometimes they are not. If we are mature, we have to unlearn any enjoyment of that power.

"You have to know that the power is there, and then you have to see if you can possibly live without it. That doesn't mean you never get into a situation where lying might be necessary but, on the whole, you try to lead your life so that you ★ communicate with other people without trying to manipulate them."
—Sissela Bok, philosopher

WE LIE THE MOST TO THOSE WE LOVE

Americans confess to having regularly lied to the following:

Person to Whom Lies Are Told	Percentage of People Who Lie
Parent	86%
Friend	75
Sibling	73
Lover	73
Spouse	69
Boss	61
Child	59
Best friend	58
Co-worker	56
Neighbor	49
Grandparent	47
Work subordinate	45
Doctor	32
Accountant	22
Clergyman	21
Lawyer	20

. . . AND THOSE WE LOVE LIE TO US

Person Who Lies to Us	Percentage Who Agree
Friend	84%
Child	83
Co-worker	80
Sibling	80
Lover	80
Spouse	78
Parent	75
Boss	72
Work subordinate	72
Best friend	68
Neighbor	67
Grandparent	49
Lawyer	42
Accountant	34
Clergyman	32
Doctor	31

We asked people about the most serious lie that had ever been told to them:

- A man from the Northwest: "That a child was mine and, three years later, it was proved he wasn't by a blood test."
- A woman from the Southeast: "That my ex-husband wasn't having sex with my daughter."
- A woman in her twenties from the Northeast: "My husband stole $1,000 from me and then lied. I found out the truth six months later."
- A man from the Midwest: "Being told my biological mother was dead, when she lived a few blocks from me."
- A woman from the South: "My second husband told me he was not a gambler, never gambled. In fact, he was a compulsive gambler. What a pig!"

As further confirmation of America's distrust of authority, 32 percent think that they've been lied to by a clergyman. The same applies to accountants (34 percent). And in the case of lawyers, people say it in spades: Forty-two percent believe that they've been lied to by attorneys.

WHAT WE LEARNED ABOUT LIARS

What are we to make of all of this lying? Here are some observations that we made, based on thousands of interviews:

- Most of our lies are relatively harmless.
- Most Americans are not trying to hurt other people with their lies.
- Lying does empower many of us. It allows us to be people we aren't. It gives us the illusion of control.
- There are more serious liars right now (liars who do harm) than at any time in our nation's past.
- Inside many liars is an honest person trying to get out. In our interviews, we let some of those people out—for a day, anyway.
- Lying has become a cultural trait in America. Lying is embedded in our national character. That hasn't really been understood around the world. Americans lie about everything—and usually for no good reason.
- The majority of Americans today (two in every three) believe that there is nothing wrong with telling a lie. Only 31 percent of us believe that honesty is the best policy.

T E S T ★ ★ ★ ★ ★ ★ ★ ★ ★ ★

Most of us are not the kind of people that others think we are. We aren't even the kind of people that *we* think we are. In this decade especially, we have set up elaborate facades to prevent others from viewing the real "us."

Do you know who you really are? What you really believe?

We invite you to answer these questions by taking the tests throughout this book.

After you finish all of the tests, you'll see how you compare to the rest of us.

Answer the yes-or-no questions below. Add up your score. Then see how you compare to the rest of the country.

ARE YOU TRUE TO YOURSELF?

1. Do you have a private life that you keep secret from others?
2. Are there sides of your life that none of your friends knows about?
3. The best of cosmetic surgeons offers you a free operation to alter any part of your face or body. Would you accept the offer?
4. You break an expensive vase in an antique store. Nobody sees you do it. Would you tell the owner?
5. Do you think that most people know "the real you"?
6. You are hooked up to a lie detector. Would you agree in advance to answer any question that your spouse or lover wanted to ask you?
7. Do you always stand up for what you believe, no matter what the consequences?
8. Do you think that your friends would be surprised if they came to know "the real you"?
9. Have you ever concealed your true feelings from your spouse or lover?
10. Do you do things that no one else knows about in the privacy of your home?
11. Do you socialize with people you really don't like?
12. Do you sometimes see yourself as a hypocrite or a phony?
13. You are losing your hair at a rapid rate. Would you consider wearing a wig or hairpiece?
14. Do you often say things that you don't mean for the sake of politeness?
15. You have an unplanned one-night stand with a stranger. Your spouse does not suspect. Would you confess?
16. Some people cannot disguise their personality for anyone or in any situation. Are you such a person?
17. Have you ever lied about your age, your income, or your education?

18. Would you tell a very close friend that he or she has bad breath?

19. Have you ever told anyone, "I love you," without meaning it?

20. Did you lie a little on the test? If so, don't you think that you'd better take it again?

Give yourself one point for any of the following questions marked Yes: 4, 5, 6, 7, 15, 16, 18.

Give yourself one point for any of the following questions marked No: 1, 2, 3, 8, 9, 10, 11, 12, 13, 14, 17, 19.

Question 20 is not scored.

Add up your score: _____ .

NATIONAL RESULTS

| Score | Percentage of the Population Who Scored | | Rating |
	Above You	Below You	
15–19	5%	95%	Honest to yourself
14	10	90	
13	20	80	
12	30	70	
11	40	60	
10	50	50	
9	60	40	Hypocrite
8	70	30	
7	80	20	
5–6	90	10	
0–4	95	5	Complete phony

5

The New American
Dreams

When he was a young stand-up comic, Woody Allen said that his greatest regret in life was that he wasn't somebody else.

Most of us had the same dream when we were kids: that we would go to sleep and when we woke up, we'd be someone else, someone magical or fantastic, someone far better than ourselves.

We asked adults to play this revealing psychological game with us, to dream their dream: How would they change themselves if they really could? How might they fulfill their potential as humans?

And what Americans said: They would be thin and they would be rich.

That is the American dream of the 1990s: Greed is okay, most Americans are saying, so long as it's not fattening.

In our respondents' dreams of their remade selves, "smarter" ran a very distant second. "Better person" didn't even finish in the rankings.

People across the country showed much less interest in changing their inner selves, including their intelligence or personality, than they did in changing their outward appearances of weight, body, hair, face, and age.

American women continue to be dissatisfied with their outward appearance. More than men, they'd change their faces and bodies and, especially (63 percent vs. 38 percent), their weight—thinner thighs, and Ben & Jerry's too!

Here's an interesting twist: It was a comic staple, before there was a George Burns, that women lie about their ages. Many people assume that it's ruder to ask women than men to tell their ages. But more men than women said that they'd change their age if they could.

Very few people (2 percent for each) want to change their race or sex. The two-thirds of those who want to change their race belong to nonwhite minorities. Blacks are more interested than Hispanics in changing race.

IF YOU COULD CHANGE ONE THING ABOUT YOURSELF, WHAT WOULD IT BE?

Aspect of Self	Percentage Who Would Change
Weight	51%
Body	32
Age	32
Intelligence	32
Height	21
Hair	20
Personality	18
Face	14
Sex	2
Race	2

IF YOU COULD CHANGE ONE THING ABOUT YOUR LIFE, WHAT WOULD IT BE?

Aspect of Life	Percentage Who Would Change
Wealth	64%
Education	45
Bad habit	45
Current job	32
Community	23
Profession	19
Sex life	19
Addiction	18
Family background	15
Marital status	15
Spouse	6
Lover	6
Friend	5
Parent	5
Child	3

WHAT MEN AND WOMEN WOULD CHANGE IF THEY COULD

Aspect	Percentage Who Would Change	
	Men	Women
Wealth	66%	61%
Weight	38	63
Body	26	39
Age	34	29
Community	26	20
Profession	22	16
Face	12	17

Most of the would-be sex-swappers (57 percent) are male. Two-thirds are under the age of forty, and they come from poverty-level households.

Men are less content with their current place in the world. More than women, they want to be better off, to change their occupation and their community.

AMERICA'S TOP FIVE BODY CHANGES

As well as being the "decade of greed," the 1980s may also be viewed as the cosmetic surgery decade with tremendous increases in all manner of cosmetic surgery procedures. The fastest-growing cosmetic surgery procedure of the 1980s was liposuction (fat removal), rising from just 1,000 operations in 1981 to an amazing 250,000 in 1989. In fact, there were more liposuction procedures in 1989 than there were combined liposuction, eyelid "tuck," breast augmentation, nose reshaping, and face-lift operations in 1981.

Cosmetic Surgery Procedure	1981	1989
Liposuction	1,000	250,000
Eyelid surgery	56,000	100,000
Breast augmentation	72,000	100,000
Nose reshaping	54,500	95,000
Face-lifts	39,000	75,000

WHAT WE LIE ABOUT

Very often, Americans lie about the identity they are trapped in. Ninety percent of Americans say that they've told harmless lies about one or more of the following aspects of themselves:

LIES WE TELL ABOUT OURSELVES

Subject of Lie	Percentage Who Have Fibbed
True feelings	81%
Income	43
Accomplishments	42
Sex life	40
Age	31
Education	23
Family background	22
Marital status	16
Race	14

It's been said that an era comes to an end when its dreams are exhausted. America's dreams are wearing extremely thin—at least the kind of dreams that can sustain a great nation.

6

The American Hall
of Shame

In each of our interviews, we peeled away defense mechanisms and began to reveal the private person, some would say the *real* person. "What are the worst things you've ever done in your life?" we asked people. "What are you ashamed of, if anything?"

Answers to these kinds of questions are barometers of what people really believe is immoral behavior, and, among various kinds of immoral acts, which are the most serious in their minds.

Equally important, the answers reveal whether people feel shame. And a number of us simply do not feel guilt or shame at all these days.

Early in each interview, we got people to talk about their doubts. Next, we asked about actions that they were *sure* were wrong—totally out of bounds—immoral.

We asked if they had done anything in the previous year of which they felt truly ashamed. About one-fourth said that they had. We then asked those people to tell us about the events or thoughts that had caused their shame.

Sex, addictions, lies, and stealing were the subjects people talked about, but their actions weren't in any gray area between right and wrong. No doubts there—they knew these were things against their personal moral code.

Sexuality creates the most problems for people:

- A churchgoing man from the West Coast: "I had sex with my mother. We did it twice, successive nights."
- "I had sex with a minor (thirteen years old)," said a cook from the Midwest. "She used to come into the restaurant for ice cream and Cokes. I've wanted to undo it for eight years."
- A divorced Midwestern baker: "I had a sexual relationship with two married men. I hurt their wives and families."
- "I became a prostitute for several months," said an East Coast saleswoman. And a Midwestern janitor in her twenties: "I was a prostitute for about three days so that I could support my drug habit." "My marriage is an act of prostitution," said a homemaker from the East Coast.
- "I had intercourse with my brother's wife. She got pregnant," said a man from the Granary region.
- "Had two abortions and didn't tell my spouse." "Had an affair, and then, because he was black, I had an abortion." "I had an abortion after I had an affair with my boyfriend's best friend."

★ | **AMERICA'S HALL OF SHAME**

What we are most ashamed of having engaged in (arguably the truest indicator of America's private morality):

Activity	Percentage Ashamed
Adultery/affair	18%
Fornication/premarital sex	14
Lying	11
Illegal drug use	10
Stealing	9
Cheating/taking advantage of others	6
Drunkenness	5
Abortion	3
Shoplifting	3
Wicked thoughts	3
Verbal cruelty	2
Masturbation	2
Stealing from work	2
Kinky sex	2
Pornography	2

Sometimes, the business world brings out the worst in people:

- A Midwestern woman, in her late sixties, married with children: "Told tales on a fellow employee. Lied to my family. Been two-faced all my life."
- "I've told bold-faced lies to employers and friends," said a salesman from the East. And a woman realtor from the West Coast, in her thirties, simply said: "I have a habit of lying at work."

Violence haunts the memories of many young males in our country:

- "Put someone in the hospital."—a young man from the Midwest. And another young man, this one an auto mechanic from the West Coast: "Throwing rocks at people. Beating up people."
- "Beating my mom," says still another young man from the Midwest.
- A Southern man, in his twenties: "Cheap, wanton sex, theft, vandal-

---

PROFILE: AMERICAN SOCIOPATH: A WEREWOLF IN PINSTRIPES

Man, in his late forties, white, third marriage, college graduate, annual household income $70,000 to 80,000, currently a stockbroker in the Rust Belt:

He calls himself a very bad man and says that if his friends knew what he is really like, they would give him up.

He obsesses about hurting women. He'll read any book on the subject and rents movies showing excessive violence.

He often thinks about torturing and killing small animals—and has frequently acted on those impulses.

The three most important reasons he married his current wife are (1) money; (2) convenience; and (3) sex. But, he says, his marital sex is boring and too infrequent, and he and his wife have nothing to talk about. The only need of his that she satisfies is financial.

He is frequently unfaithful. He has had seven affairs during this marriage. Among the women are strangers, old flames, and, currently, a local bartender.

He says that he feels not the slightest guilt about his infidelities.

Men and women don't respect each other, in his opinion. Women are money-grubbers. Men are vicious and most of them are repressed killers, in his opinion. He saw that to be true in wartime.

He has taken many drugs, among them LSD, cocaine, PCP, and methadone. He started the drug-taking while in the Air Force.

He has stolen from his parents, co-workers, bosses, friends, lovers, and neighbors.

His personal values are his alone. He says that no other person and no institution had any influence on how he became who he is.

ism, petty lies." And a Northeastern construction worker in his thirties: "Stolen, lied, shot a woman, utilized drugs, and attempted suicide."

T E S T II ★ ★ ★ ★ ★ ★ ★ ★ ★ ★

We can tell you, most people think that they are good people. But are they really? Are you?

We all have a fair idea of what makes a person good and, of course, every religion sets down certain standards to live by. But it's not always easy to tell how well we do at following the standards, much less to know how others are doing. Here's a test we gave across the country. By taking it yourself, you can find out where you fit on a scale that ranges from saint to sociopath. Answer the yes-or-no questions, then add up your score. Are you a better person—or a worse one—than you think you are?

ARE YOU REALLY A GOOD PERSON?

1. Would you take on full responsibility for the care of your aging parents?
2. You see a child, whom you don't know, run in front of a moving car. Would you risk your life to save the child by jumping in front of the car yourself?
3. Have you ever done any volunteer work or community service?
4. Would you object if the authorities announced their intention to locate a homeless shelter in your neighborhood?
5. If your best friend lost his or her job and home, would you take him or her in?
6. You win $20 million in a lottery. Would you give half of it to charity?
7. The only thing that can save the life of your brother or sister is one of your kidneys. Would you donate it?
8. Part of the taxes you pay supports welfare programs for the poor. Do you approve of this?
9. Do you donate 10 percent or more of your annual income to charitable causes?
10. Would you take a 10 percent pay cut if it would save the jobs of the people you work with?
11. Convicted drug dealers, rapists, and murderers are entitled to protection from cruel and unusual punishment. Do you agree?
12. Have you ever willingly taken the blame for someone else?

13. You find a wallet stuffed with $100 bills and the owner's address. Would you keep the money?
14. If you could get your boss's job by telling what you know about his or her personal life, would you do it?
15. You see someone being attacked on the street. You are the only other person in sight. Would you physically intervene?
16. Is there anyone for whose life you would give up your own?
17. Your spouse or lover is dying of cancer. Would you spend all of your savings to ease his or her last days?
18. A couple who are your closest friends die in an accident. Would you take on the responsibility of raising their five-year-old child?
19. Do you give money to people begging on the street?
20. Have you ever intentionally embarrassed, insulted, or humiliated anyone?
21. Have you ever cheated anyone out of anything you consider important?

Give yourself one point for any of the following questions marked Yes: 1, 2, 3, 5, 6, 7, 8, 9, 10, 11, 12, 15, 16, 17, 18, 19.

Give yourself one point for any of the following questions marked No: 4, 13, 14, 20, 21.

Add up your score: _____ .

NATIONAL RESULTS

| | Percentage of the Population Who Scored | | |
Score	Above You	Below You	Rating
18–21	5%	95%	Saint
17	10	90	
16	20	80	
15	30	70	
14	40	60	
13	50	50	
12	60	40	
11	70	30	
10	80	20	
8–9	90	10	
0–7	95	5	Sociopath

7

Some Really Good People in America

There's a lot of cynicism right now about this country. It would be misleading to suggest that Americans are bad people at this point in history, or that there aren't a lot of wonderful people in the United States, because there are. We interviewed some of them, and we heard about others.

First, some generalities about the goodness of Americans (we'll expand on much of this in later chapters):

1. Religion appears to play a strong role in building moral character. We found that people who defined themselves as religious showed a much stronger commitment to moral values and social institutions than did nonreligious people.

2. Women are by far the more moral sex across a broad range of areas.

3. American workers are far more moral than managers are. They act much more ethically in the workplace. They say that they do—but so do the managers.

4. The older we are, the less likely we are to commit what we know to be immoral acts.

★ PEOPLE WHO HAVE TOLD THEMSELVES, "EVERYBODY DOES THAT" AND THEN
HAVE DONE SOMETHING IMMORAL

Age Group	Percentage Who Agree
18–24	64%
25–44	55
45–64	41
65 and older	30

★ WHO IS GOOD IN AMERICA?

Are there ways to identify groups of good people? Do groups of us believe in our
hearts that we are the good people? It seems that way.

People Who Describe Themselves as "Very Good"

Group	Percentage Who Agree
Jews	41%
The elderly (ages 65 and older)	35
College-educated	35
Blacks	34
Catholics	30
Homosexuals	30
Whites	28
Protestants	27
Liberals	26
Ages 18–24	25

DID OUR PARENTS HELP?

We asked people to tell us what portion of their current values they
received from their parents. The result: The role that we believe our
parents play in shaping values and good people in our society is definitely
declining:

Only 50 percent of eighteen- to twenty-four-year-olds honestly feel that
they've gotten a strong moral foundation from their parents vs. 61 percent
of adults aged twenty-five to sixty vs. 78 percent of Americans aged sixty-
five or older.

SOME GOOD PEOPLE IN AMERICA

Good People in Hollywood

As far as honesty goes, Hollywood takes a few shots in the media and usually deserves them. On the other hand, there are many people in movieland who have very fine reputations. Here are some of Hollywood's best people, according to samplings we did in Los Angeles and New York. These are not national surveys.

Meryl Streep—actress
Paul Newman—actor
Robert Redford—actor/director
Howard Koch—past president, Motion Picture Academy
Alan Ladd—Chairman/CEO, Pathé Films
Grant Tinker—TV producer
Bernie Brillstein—manager and Jim Henson's partner
Fred DeCordova—producer, *The Tonight Show*
Talia Shire—actress
Carol Burnett—actress
Audrey Hepburn—actress

Good People in Washington

We asked people in Washington about the good people at work in our capital.

Thomas Eagleton—former U.S. Senator, Missouri
Bill Bradley—U.S. Senator, New Jersey
Sam Nunn—U.S. Senator, Chairman of Senate Armed Services Committee
Elizabeth Dole—former member, U.S. Cabinet
Sandra Day O'Connor—Supreme Court Justice
Barbara Bush—First Lady
Howard Baker—former U.S. Senator and White House Chief of Staff
George Mitchell—U.S. Senator, Maine
Paul Sarbanes—U.S. Senator, Maryland

Good People in Business

Business people were asked about the good people they've had dealings with.

Peter Grace—W. R. Grace
Richard Jenrette—Equitable Life
Robert Crandall—American Airlines
Sam Walton—Wal-Mart Stores
John Akers—IBM
John Sculley—Apple Computer
Roy Vagelos—Merck and Co.
James Burke—Johnson & Johnson
David Kearns—Xerox
Beverly Dolan—Textron

Good People in Sports

We talked to sports writers and coaches about athletes, especially star athletes.

Bobby Ojeda—New York Mets (baseball)
Barry Sanders—Detroit Lions (football)
Michael Chang—tennis professional
Joe Montana—San Francisco 49ers (football)
Carl Banks—New York Giants (football)
Don Mattingly—New York Yankees (baseball)
Dale Murphy—Philadelphia Phillies (baseball)
Nolan Ryan—Houston Astros (baseball)
Mike Schmidt—Philadelphia Phillies (baseball; retired)
Larry Bird—Boston Celtics (basketball)

Most impressive of all, however, is the current desire of Americans to give of themselves, to give time and money, to give whatever it takes to fix some of the current problems in America. Fully half of all Americans are now ready and available for volunteer work in this country. For more good news, see Chapter 34.

In Chapter 8, however, we will consider something else, an offer that most Americans couldn't seem to refuse.

8

<hr>

What Are You Willing to Do for $10 Million? For $2 Million?

<hr>

We're good people, if we say so ourselves—and we generally do.

But for *$10 million*? Does that change anything? Does cold cash change our morals? It is a pivotal question in a money-oriented society. So we asked it in every interview.

Sure enough, money talked to people across the country. For $10 million, one in four of us would abandon all of our friends or abandon our church. About as many would turn to prostitution for a week. Some of us would go much farther—as far as murder, changing their race, or a sex-change operation.

In fact, 7 percent of us say they would murder someone for money. That's about one in every fourteen people. Whether they could actually pull the trigger is another question, but 36 million of us would be willing to consider the offer.

We did a follow-up telephone survey to our $10-million question. The results remained pretty much the same at $5 million, at $4 million, and at $3 million.

Under $2 million is where we began to see a fall-off in what people are willing to do. Our price in America seems to be $2 million or thereabouts.

✶ | **WHAT ARE YOU HONESTLY WILLING TO DO FOR $10 MILLION?**

We asked people if they would do any of the following for $10 million. Two-thirds of them would agree to at least one, some to several.

Would abandon their entire family (25 percent)
Would abandon their church (25 percent)
Would become prostitutes for a week or more (23 percent)
Would give up their American citizenship (16 percent)
Would leave their spouses (16 percent)
Would withhold testimony and let a murderer go free (10 percent)
Would kill a stranger (7 percent)
Would change their race (6 percent)
Would have a sex-change operation (4 percent)
Would put their children up for adoption (3 percent)

✶ | **BY REGION: WHERE THE SOCIOPATHS LIVE**

(For a map of America's regions, see Part I.)

Our interviews revealed a number of people without much if any conscience—people known as sociopaths. Sociopaths are found in varying proportions around the country, but more so in the Pacific Northwest.

WHO THE SOCIOPATHS ARE (National Average: 11%)

Region	Percentage Who Are Sociopaths
Pac Rim	22%
Marlboro Country	16
New South	16
New England	14
Metropolis	12
Rust Belt	11
Granary	9
L.A.–Mex	7
Old Dixie	5

Sociopaths and *Twin Peaks*

Twin Peaks may be accurate after all. On the TV show *Twin Peaks*, a small northwestern town is the site of all kinds of seedy and unconscionable activities. According to our data, film director David Lynch's vision may not be far from the truth. Pac Rim respondents were much less likely to have strongly developed consciences than were individuals in any other area. In fact, in our testing, they were four times as likely to be sociopaths as were citizens of Old Dixie and nearly twice as likely as were those perennial suspects from Metropolis.

Coupled with the observation that Pac Rimmers are the regional respondents least likely to present themselves to others as they really are, it seems that David Lynch may be on to something.

IV

THE
SEX
LIVES
OF
AMERICANS

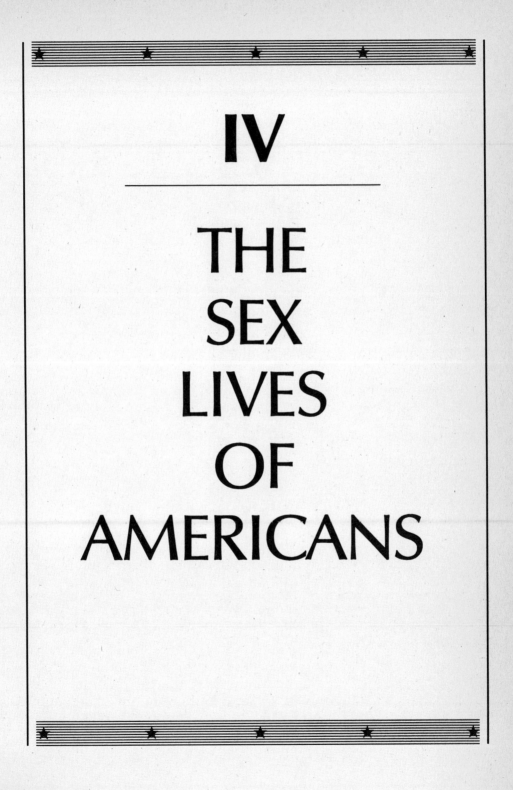

IV

THE
SEX
LIVES
OF
AMERICANS

9

After Kinsey, Masters and Johnson, and the Hite Reports

A lot has happened to our sexual mores since Kinsey, Masters and Johnson, and Hite published their first books. A lot has happened to us since the appearance of AIDS. Here's what we found out about what's going on behind the bedroom doors of today's Americans.

AMERICANS CAN'T GET ENOUGH

If sex were an expensive restaurant, contemporary Americans would give it a rating of two and a half stars out of four: good eats, but skimpy portions. Our sex lives are actually pretty good, but we want more. This sexual hunger leads us to places and practices where the Bible and many federal and state laws explicitly tell us not to go. We couldn't care less.

Most Americans are not hard up for sex. Indeed, from the figures we have, the average American can expect to enjoy more sex with more partners for more years than any other people in history. By quite a lot, too.

Sex, for the majority of Americans, is available for the asking.

So who's complaining? Two in every three men, and half of the women, said they wished that they could spend more time making love—but not with their current lovers.

No matter who they're doing it with, a very large number of Americans deny that there is such a thing as enough sex. Fully one-fourth (30 percent of men, 19 percent of women) describe their sexual appetite as "insatiable."

It may never be enough, but some of the Insatiables manage to have sex several times a day.

WHO'S GOTTA HAVE IT?

Homosexuals and bisexuals are twice as likely as the average person to have multiple daily sex. Young people (eighteen- to twenty-four-year-olds), single people, divorced people: All scored above the average. Liberals are twice as likely as conservatives to make love more than once a day.

SEX BY THE CLOCK

Statement	Percentage Who Agree
I wish I could spend more time making love	58%
I spend just the right amount of time making love	36
I wish I could spend less time making love	3
I hate the thought of making love	4

SEX: MEN WANT IT MORE!

Statement	Percentage Who Agree
I think that men enjoy sex more than women do	46%
I think that women enjoy sex more than men do	20
I think that men can live without sex	24
I think that women can live without sex	44

In terms of the idealized couple of the past—virgins joined in holy matrimony, faithful till death do them part—we found nothing but a shadow on the wall.

Ninety-two percent of sexually active people report having had ten or more lovers, with a lifetime average of seventeen. Four in ten among us have had more than one lover in the past year. Singles get around much more. Since they became sexually active (by the age of sixteen for the majority), single people have averaged a four-above-par twenty-one lovers, four in the last year.

Despite its high overall rating (eight on a scale of one to ten), sex in America isn't always so great. When people told us what they dislike about sex with their current lover or spouse, there was a lengthy list of sexual grievances, many of them emotional.

AMERICA'S TEN TOP SEXUAL COMPLAINTS

Here are America's ten most popular sexual complaints:

- *Rejection*: "When she says, 'No,' it breaks my heart. It makes me feel like I'm nothing." "He rolls over and I cry myself to sleep."
- *Not enough*: "He gets tired too fast. I want to go twenty minutes, at least." "We don't have sex a lot. He's a sailor, so he's out to sea. We can't be alone enough to enjoy it." "She has all these Roman-Catholic hang-ups. Stay away from Irish-Catholic girls."
- *Too fast*: "When it's over too quickly, I feel terribly used, like a disposable lover." "Actual intercourse doesn't last long enough. It never has." "Quick sex is no good. He doesn't last when he's drunk." "She quits early, doesn't really like sex with me." "He doesn't take his time getting me hot." "He gets aroused faster than me. Then he gets unaroused a *lot* faster than me."
- *Too slow*: For some women: "He does it for an hour. He's so long-winded in erection." For some men also: "She's more than I can handle sometimes. Some nights I'm very tired and want to go to sleep, but she'll want to keep on doing it." "She likes triathlons in bed. Maybe she's trying to kill me?"
- *Medical problems*: "Dry vagina." "Hemorrhoids for both of us." "It hurts when he enters me." "I think one day she's going to break it off. She calls it her joystick."
- *Unskilled partner*: "I have a terrible lover. He feels inadequate—not polished or knowing in how to satisfy." "He wants me to be exciting

even when I don't feel like it. He expects a Vegas showgirl," said a woman from the Southwest in her twenties.

- *Sex is just boring*: "Same place, same time, same channel," says a nurse from the Midwest. "Old hat. You've seen it, you've seen it— and I've seen it," according to a fisherman from the East Coast.
- *No good foreplay* (women's most common complaint): "I don't like his foreplay. He has plumbers' hands." "He doesn't know how to use his tongue. His tongue's as useless as tits on a bull." "No foreplay, zero. Sometimes he is too slam-bam impatient." "Usually, he doesn't want to do foreplay and get me as aroused as he is. Four out of five times it's like that."
- *Lack of afterglow* (women's next biggest complaint): "He usually just rolls over and conks out afterwards." This was said by a twenty-one-year-old single woman, who has had thirty lovers since she lost her virginity at the age of fifteen.
- *Bad timing* (another common complaint among women): "He wants to have sex only when he wants. It's rarely, if ever, at *my* convenience." "Often, he's ready but I'm not." "Sometimes, he's not ready when I am." "When he wants it in the morning, which is every morning, he's like a bad alarm clock."
- People got pretty graphic at times with their descriptions: "She farts too much." "Bad breath." "He doesn't brush his teeth." "His body odor, when he doesn't take a bath." "We are both a hundred pounds overweight." "She's no Madonna." "He isn't exactly Johnny Depp."
- Still another frequent issue between the sexes is the partner who goes too far—or not far enough: "She's got this long list of things she absolutely will not do. Everything is against her freaking religion." "He has this fascination with sodomy." "She needs a lot of foreplay, and she won't let me come in her mouth." "Swallowing it, she won't." "He tries to perform anal sex, and I think it's both wrong and dangerous. I don't really know where he's had that thing—not even that day."

SOME PEOPLE HAD NO COMPLAINTS ABOUT SEX

Fifteen percent of adult Americans would rather watch television.

10

Sex, American Style: Fact and Fantasy

Americans' sexual fantasies are original and creative. Just when we thought that we'd seen and heard it all, along came someone whose admitted sexual fantasy is unique.

Men and women of all ages told us their sexual fantasies, some of which they had never told their own spouses.

We found Americans of all ages, all walks of life—traffic cops and legal secretaries, fast-food managers and high fashion models, doctors and truck drivers—making it on top of cars and on pirate ships and in roller coasters and immersed in Jell-O and at the 50-yard line and handcuffed or blindfolded or kidnapped and beating or licking or tickling one or two or several partners of the same or the opposite sex and race and sometimes of another species altogether and once of no species at all.

WHAT'S LOVE GOT TO DO WITH IT?

Where to begin? Well, sex with famous people is our second most popular fantasy (after oral sex):

75

- A married man from the East, who rated his sex life as "completely satisfactory," nonetheless could dream: "I pile all of the nude Miss Americas on top of me and let myself work through them all."
- An office manager from the Midwest, in her forties, imagined herself: "On an island paradise like Curaçao with Robert Redford."
- The location didn't matter to a woman from the South, married, so long as the company was right: "To fuck Mel Gibson anywhere, anytime, for about two weeks uninterrupted. I see his cute little butt all the time in my daydreams."
- A single woman in her twenties, from the Midwest: "To have girl-sex with Madonna for forty-eight hours and get paid for my services. Cha, cha, cha."
- The composer of the *B-Minor Mass* would surely be bemused to find himself cast in the high-tech fantasy of a woman from the Southwest, who said that she is addicted to sex and shopping: "A sheetless waterbed, Wesson oil, a strobe light, and the music of [Johann] Sebastian Bach."
- Among the other celebrities listed in these forays of the imagination are: "Sex with Big Mike Ditka." "Being in mad love with Stacey Keach and Michael Keaton." "Screwing Brandi Brandt." "Nicole Eggert." "Debbie Gibson." "Linda Carter." "Bon Jovi." (Several people chose the hard-rock star). "George Bush in the White House bedroom."

★ | **WHAT MEN WANT IN BED!**

If there's any doubt about what men want in bed, our data should end the speculation: Men want oral sex! Three in four American men confess to fantasizing about it.

At a time when greed is celebrated, it is only fitting that sexual greed in the form of the harem—a lot of them for one of me—should be popular in our fantasies. Have men really changed and become more sensitized? It doesn't show up here. They still want multiple sex parts—and multiple partners:

- A male truck driver from the South saw it in its classic version: "To be treated like a king and have a harem of women to do with as I please."

- For a married electronic technician from the East Coast, in his thirties, it went like this: "Simply put: two (maybe three) beautiful—perfect!—women and me!"
- It was on the road, with exclamation marks, for a young man from the West Coast: "Three women pick me up and take me on a trip for two weeks—the time of my life!!!"

Nowadays, a lot of women own harems, too—at least in their dreams:

- A secretary in her fifties, from the East, addicted to food and shopping, but not to sex, nonetheless imagined: "Three men and me. A harem of men—one for each pleasure—from top to bottom."
- A housewife in her twenties, from the South, had: "Two to three men make love to me all at once. They do whatever I want."
- A secretary from the Midwest, married, in her thirties, saw it happen-

---

THE TWENTY-THREE SEX FANTASIES AMERICANS HAVE MOST

Fantasy	Percentage	
	Men	Women
Oral sex	75%	43%
Sex with a famous person	59	39
Multiple partners	57	24
Sex with someone of another race	52	25
Using sexual devices	38	29
Sex in a public place	39	26
Swapping partners	42	15
Sex with a much younger person	39	15
Sex with a fictional TV character	30	20
Sex with a teenager	42	8
Sex with a much older person	34	15
Sex with dominance/submission	27	19
Anal sex	39	14
Being a porno star	30	10
Calling a telephone sex line	20	7
Sex with a physical object	15	11
Sadomasochistic sex	12	7
Sex mixed with violence	13	4
Incest	13	3
Sex with an animal	8	3
Sex with urination	8	3
Sex with a child	8	2
Sex with defecation	5	1

ing at the office: "On my desk. One man I like behind me, squeezing boobs. Another man I know giving me oral sex."

There are gay harems:

- A man from the South, in his thirties, had: "One hundred well-oiled football players at my beck and call for a week on a yacht."
- A married man from Los Angeles, who described himself as bisexual, wanted: "To be surrounded by twenty of the best-looking males and to be sexually abused by all."

Power in its various sexual manifestations is the central element in many fantasies:

- A truck driver from the Midwest saw: "Three girls, two tied up, me and one girl going at the other two."
- A young man from the East said: "Anal sex with my wife in submission."
- A young stock clerk from the Midwest imagined: "Being handcuffed and pissed on."
- A young truck driver from the Midwest said: "Wearing her underwear for humiliation's sake."

The dark, handsome corsairs of Gothic fiction still find their way into the dreams of many American women:

- A divorced woman in her fifties, from the Southwest: "A pirate overpowering me. I put up a good struggle, but I wanted him all the time."
- Similarly, a married woman from the West Coast, thirties, said: "Sex with a pirate captain on board a sailing ship."
- In the dreams of a woman computer specialist from the Southwest, married, thirties: "Being kidnapped by a sheik and taken to his tent and having sex. We marry and live in his palace."
- A white man from the East revealed: "I want to make love to a black woman on a mountain trail on a spring day."
- A male manager from the East Coast, white, twenties: "Two Chinese girls at one time."
- A white market research interviewer from the West Coast, a man in his forties, said: "Being with a group of Asian women and having all of them make love to me."
- An interracial mixer for a young white man from the East: "Being

on a beach in Florida and having girls from different worlds make love to me."

Food made its way into hundreds of the sexual fantasies we heard about. Maybe dinner–massage parlors are coming next?

- "Make love in a pool of Jell-O." "Taking a bath in chocolate Jell-O pudding." "To do it in a bathtub full of vanilla pudding." "To be covered in whipped cream and wrestle my lover, then the loser has to lick it off." "Oral sex with whipping cream." "Having sex with sliced peaches involved."

A lot of Americans want to play to an audience:

- A Midwesterner in his early forties dreamed of: "Having a woman sitting on my face on top of the Sears Building."
- A young man from the Southeast: "Having sex on the fifty-yard line at a sold-out football game."

And old-fashioned romance still fills many of our fantasies—in fact, romance has become a fantasy for a lot of men and women:

- A personnel director from the Southwest imagined that she will: "Dress up in wonderful clothes and seduce him in the living room, bedroom."
- For a sales clerk from the East, in her early forties, it was: "A sexy attractive man running after me on the beach at night."
- And a computer consultant, a man from the East: "Perfect, romantic seduction by a gorgeous, healthy, uninhibited woman."
- And these standards: "Making love on New Year's Eve—chilled wine, champagne, and soft music." "I am waltzing with some handsome man—wined, dined, romanced." "Having a fireplace and, after dinner, making love all night." "A very strong yet tender man comes to my rescue when I am in need of help."
- The golden years, as imagined by a golden girl in her late sixties from the Midwest: "Sleazy sex with an old man."

SEX WITH RABBITS?

Last, and maybe least, a young man from the Southwest: He confides that his only addiction is to sex and said that he has dreams of "having sex with Jessica Rabbit." Never mind that she is a cartoon!

THE TRUTH BEHIND CLOSED DOORS

We had believed that not much in the real world could live up to people's sexual fantasies.

Not so. When people recounted their *actual* sexual experiences, their reality often topped the imaginary events of their fantasies.

If we can dream it up, we just might do it. And most Americans, the *majority* of us, have acted out real-life versions of our sexual fantasies.

So much so, in fact, that many experiences now seem, if not normal, at least far less bizarre than they once did. As a Midwestern grade school teacher said of anal sex: "Rear entry isn't even close to kinky today. It's five on a scale of [one to] ten."

Of course, Americans have not visited all of the wilder shores of love they've glimpsed in their fantasies. Not one person reported being kidnapped by a pirate captain, and no one owned up to a harem of well-oiled football players.

But here's what they *have* done.

THEY "DID IT"

- An executive, a man from the Midwest, married, in his thirties, did it: "Hot wax, Jell-O, two girls, and one of their dogs."
- An accountant from the East, in his twenties, did it: "Some fraternity brothers, a half-keg of beer, several sheep."
- "I let my standard poodle lick me until I come," said a single woman from the Midwest.
- "My husband, his best friend, and I slept together for about a year and a half," said a store manager from the Southwest. "The friend and I began making love while my husband was asleep."

Millions of Americans have experienced sexual multiple plays, according to the statistics:

- A secretary from the Midwest, single, in her twenties: "I was with two men at once for a week at Lake Tahoe." A sales associate from the East Coast, single, in her twenties: "Two strange men and me in the back of a pickup truck in Ocean City."
- A divorced man in his sixties, from the South, remembered: "Sex with six people in bed."
- Another respondent said: "An orgy with about twenty people."
- A young bisexual telephone company operator recalled: "A homosexual daisy chain. This happened frequently one summer in Manhattan."

THE FUTURE OF SEX

"What's sex going to be in the 1990s? It's going to be you—and you."
—Robin Williams

CHASTITY

"It's the most unnatural of the sexual perversions."
—Aldous Huxley

LIVING OUT OUR FANTASIES: THE TOP TWENTY-THREE

Here's how many people have actually realized their sexual fantasies.

Reality	Percentage	
	Men	Women
Oral sex	79%	70%
Masturbation	73	53
Anal sex	40	34
Using sexual devices	32	31
Sex in a public place	37	25
Sex games	38	23
Sex with someone of another race	42	18
Sex with a much older person	30	16
Sex with a teenager	35	8
Sex with a much younger person	28	10
Multiple partners	31	10
Sex with dominance/submission	22	14
Calling a telephone sex line	23	6
Sex with someone of the same sex	17	11
Swapping partners	20	6
Sex with a physical object	12	11
Sex with violence	12	7
Sadomasochistic sex	10	6
Sex with urination	10	4
Incest	8	4
Sex with an animal	7	3
Sex with a child	6	2
Sex with defecation	5	2

Unlike fantasy, which is endlessly adaptable and which other people cannot spoil for us, the real thing can sometimes be disappointing:

- A divorced woman from the Southwest, in her fifties, had this to recount: "A threesome—another female and a male. It left a lot to be desired, so I left both of them."
- The edibles were not always good to the last drop: "I had sex in a tub of cherry Jell-O. It wasn't as much fun as it sounds."
- On the other hand: "Putting whipped cream on my partner and eating it off." "Having champagne poured on me and consumed." "I was covered head to toe with whipped cream and engaged in oral activities." "Rich's whipped cream and rubbers." "Fucking in grape Jell-O."
- Then there's this food experience: "I once, as a youth, put syrup on my penis and had flies walk on it."

A great many people confessed that they have played games that involved sex and power:

- A secretary from the South: "I tied up my boss from the factory. I kept him tied a little longer than he wanted."
- A school teacher from the East, in her thirties: "Being spanked, then 'raped,' by my husband."
- A young man from the East Coast: "Handcuffing a girl and whipping her."
- A secretary from the Midwest: "Being tied up by my spouse. We do that one once or twice a month."
- A married salesman from the Midwest: "A girl suggested I tie her to the bedposts spread-eagle. Then we could make love."
- More gently for a young married woman from the Midwest: "Tied up with laces and silk scarves."
- Men usually play the aggressor's role in these games, but not always: "Tied my spouse to the bedpost, tickled and teased him, performed oral sex on him." "I was tied to a bed while my girl friend had sex with me." "I whipped him." "Getting on top of him and riding him like a horsie."

The search for privacy accounts for some but not all of the strange places in which people have found themselves while having sex:

- A young printer from the South, in his twenties: "Making love in a chicken coop."

- A nineteen-year-old woman from the Southwest: "In a cloak closet of my high school."
- A disk jockey from the Midwest, single: "In the rest room at a downtown movie theater during a crummy movie called *Always*."

Some people had sex on commercial air flights, especially night flights.

- And these reports: "Jerking each other off in public under a table in a restaurant."—reported by a young man from the East.
- From a Navy officer from the South, married, thirties: "In a graveyard."
- The venues people find are endless: "On my roof in broad daylight." "Small closet." "On a big, round plastic slide." "In our crawlspace." "On the open balcony of a hotel in Bangkok." "In a completely open field with houses all around." "On the porch of the university chancellor's house." "In the can at school." "School gymnasium in broad daylight." "In a public park at noon. No one could see us, but we could see them."

There's an old saying that we have a love affair with the automobile:

- An executive administrator from the East, in her forties, reported that she: "Masturbated through five states, sitting in a car with no clothes on. Yahoo—those were the days!"
- Other cases of love on wheels: "On top of a car." "Front seat of a Beetle." "Back seat." "Drive-in." "Gave head to my partner driving down [Route] 51." "Oral sex while driving." "While husband was driving." "Sex in a moving car with the driver." "With this cute taxi driver."

Several reported anal intercourse with no mention of the risk of AIDS.

- A Navy veteran: "I screwed this woman in the rear, while she used a vibrator."
- A young man from the South: "Anal sex, no protection, it was crazy but fun."
- Others: "Anal sex with the aid of a device, while having intercourse." "Had anal sex, and then finished him off in my mouth." "Let someone fuck me in the butt."

Overwhelmingly, the American attitude toward sex (anything except sex with children) has become: Just do it. We are living in a time of tremendous sexual experimentation, even sexual revolution. We feel far less guilty about sexual matters than we've ever felt before.

Marlene Dietrich may have said it best: "In America, sex is an obsession. In other parts of the world, it is a fact."

V

MEN
AND
WOMEN
IN THE
1990s

11

The War Between the
Sexes Continues

THE BIG CHILL

Men and women, what's *really* going on between the sexes?

The bottom-line answer we got was "*Brrrrr.*"

Or as Charles Bukowski, the writer whose life was the basis for the movie *Barfly*, put it, "It's possible to love a human being, if you don't know them too well."

In the 1990s, men and women are meeting in a vacuum. They feel, almost universally, that they can't communicate with each other. There is distrust and bitterness between the sexes, and it's operating right on the surface.

As you'll see, the old-fashioned customs that once regulated relationships are on their way out. But nothing has taken their place. So men and women feel themselves groping, lost in their new freedom, their new roles.

One thing was clear in our interviews: Fewer men and women believe in the institution of marriage as the way to define what happens between them. Love can be defined in other ways nowadays. Living together has gained acceptance with a majority of Americans (over 50 percent).

Another signal of change: "Failure to communicate," the inability to talk to each other, is what both men and women now say is the single most important cause of American divorces.

When you actually listen to men and women talk from the heart, it becomes obvious that there are solutions. Both sexes want the same things from each other. Women want men to open up their ears and listen, to open up their hearts and understand who women are and what they need. Men want women to do the same for them.

A Midwestern male said to us, "From the time they're little girls, a lot of women are taught that they're softer, more vulnerable, meant to be mothers. Whether we like that or not, it happens. It still happens. With boys, it's drilled into their heads early that they'll have the responsibility to raise families. If they're not very good at something, they'll be considered failures in life. If you understand these differences, I think you become more tolerant, no matter which sex you are."

If women only understood men and why they are the way they are . . .

If men only understood women . . .

This should be a subject in our schools: Understanding People 101. Another course would be the next subject we explored with men and women: their honest opinion of marriage.

WHAT MEN AND WOMEN *REALLY* BELIEVE ABOUT MARRIAGE

Marriage in the 1990s just doesn't mean what it always used to mean. This is true across America in every single region.

The picture we got is that the majority of men and women aren't sure why they got married or whether they did the right thing. They're skeptical about the future of their marriages and even more so about the marriages of other people they know.

The majority of men and women now believe in their hearts that it's a good idea to live together before marriage.

Almost half of all Americans take that thought one step further: nearly half of us say that there is no reason to ever get married. And even when children are involved, only 32 percent of us believe that we should try to stick out a bad marriage for the sake of the kids.

Divorce, in fact, is what will happen to most marriages: Forty-four percent of us agree that most marriages will end in divorce.

And this fact may gladden the hearts of some lawyers: A thumping 59 percent of all Americans believe that it's a smart idea to draw up a prenuptial agreement, just in case.

One surprising statistic we discovered is that the rate of virgin marriages is highest in Metropolis, the region that includes the sophisticated and worldly cities of New York and Washington. Thirty-six percent of Metropolitans were virgins on their wedding days vs. the national average of 29 percent. At the opposite end are the Pac Rim and Marlboro Country, where only one in five are virgins at marriage.

Americans used to have the reputation of marrying for love, whereas people in other lands married for family connections, dowries, or other, more worldly reasons. Not any more: Only one in three Americans gave love as their primary reason for marrying.

★ | PROFILE: MARRIED IN THE NEW SOUTH

Woman, in her mid-thirties, white, married with children, college graduate, lives in the New South:

★ She thinks constantly of having an affair and has a few "choice possibilities" in mind. One is her family doctor, who she knows "has a wild crush on me." She and the doctor have kissed once, at a party.

She says that she is lucky in life. She loves her children, loves the time she spends at her club. The women at her club, her friends, also talk about having affairs. They rate the more attractive men and sometimes plot out ways to get them.

★ She feels that her husband is basically good, but not as worthwhile as she thought he was at one time. He is obsessed with his business, and regularly puts in a 60-hour work week, sometimes more. He thinks it's part of the job to entertain frequently at home. In this, she is treated as "one of his employees."

She feels that her current obsession with fooling around is rather adolescent, but also harmless. She has thought about divorce but, in her husband's lingo, "It doesn't make business sense."

★ She views her parents' marriage as "comfortable and perfectly dreadful." She has considered suicide, but not seriously. Another dalliance.

★ | BY REGION: VIRGIN ON WEDDING NIGHT

(For a map of America's regions, see Part I.)

VIRGIN WHEN MARRIED (National Average: 29%)

Region	Percentage	Region	Percentage
Metropolis	36%	New South	24%
Granary	33	L.A.–Mex	24
Old Dixie	32	Pac Rim	21
New England	31	Marlboro Country	21
Rust Belt	29		

Instead of love, we offer a wide variety of reasons why we marry. What's notable is the relatively low importance given to having children— and even less to sex. The latter undoubtedly reflects today's easy access to sex outside marriage.

Suppose that you could do it over again? More than half say that they would marry the same person again.

On the other hand, close to one in five say that they definitely wouldn't, and one quarter aren't sure. More than one in four are not sure that they loved the other person at the time they were married or that they do so today.

WHAT'S MISSING FROM YOUR MARRIAGE?

We asked the people we interviewed to talk about their needs, as well as the most important things missing from their marriages.

- A woman from the South wished that her spouse of ten years would "be my friend and talk and go places with me. Just laughing together. That's what I miss so much."
- A laboratory technician in her early sixties, who married her first lover thirty-five years ago and had known no others, had the very simplest of wishes: "I could use a daily hug, but I never get it. Isn't that sad?"
- Some people were simply bored by their spouses' minds. A home-maker from the West Coast said: "I'm smarter and have more interests and hobbies than he does. My husband's very regulated in his ways."
- Many women need to be more certain about their spouses' feelings. A homemaker from the Southwest, in her fifties, who married her

---

THE REASONS THAT WE MARRY IN THE 1990s

Reason	Percentage Who Agreed	Reason	Percentage Who Agreed
Love	36%	Desire to be happy	9%
Need for companionship/ fear of growing old alone	14	Money	5
		Habit/convenience	5
Desire to have children	12	Dependence	3
Sex	10	Fear of AIDS	2

very first lover: "He doesn't talk about how he feels, not to me, but especially not to his children."

- Other women said: "Communication: we don't talk about things that are important." "He doesn't share his feelings." "Conversation." "Everyday talk." "To know that I am loved and wanted." "My need to be assured that he loves me, even that he likes me."

Men's complaints were much more often about sex. Once again, this was true in every region:

- "Her sexual drive is at an all-time low," a man in his late twenties said of his wife of a year. He has thought of having an affair but hasn't actually done so.
- A student from the West Coast, addicted to food as well as to sex, missed: "Excitement, stimulation, all the nasty stuff."
- A man from Marlboro Country, in his thirties, who married his first lover and has been faithful to her, said: "There is no real excitement anymore. It's just rote and routine."

DIVORCE

Twentieth Century Fox, the studio that distributed *The War of the Roses*, was concerned that adults might find the hit movie's ending too harsh and unrealistic. Most adults didn't. Most adults are way ahead of the movie studios.

Jonathan Rose (Michael Douglas) said in the movie, "No, I think I need—I think you owe me after this many pretty damn good years of marriage a better reason than that. I work my ass off to provide a good life for you. So you owe me an answer that makes sense. Let's hear it. Let's hear it. Come on. Let's hear it."

Barbara Rose (Kathleen Turner) said: "Because . . . when I watch you eat . . . when I see you asleep . . . when I look at you . . . lately . . . I just want to smash your face in."

Real people who go through a messy divorce have their own reasons.

Communication problems are the number one reason for divorce in the 1990s. As we found out, women don't really understand men, and men don't really understand women. We heard comments such as these: "My husband was super critical and refused to communicate." "My wife and I were not communicating." "My husband was a hundred percent inattentive and thought only of himself." "I was dismally unhappy sexually—lack of communication—no trust." "He doesn't understand who I am." "She doesn't know me."

Infidelity (the other person's, of course!) ranked second. Most divorced wives (54 percent) revealed that their husbands strayed—but almost half (46 percent) of the husbands pointed a knowing finger at former wives. There are a lot of Strays out there across America:

"I found out from my hairdresser that my husband was cheating on me." "My wife was unfaithful with at least two other men." "I thought she was possibly cheating on me." "I left because my spouse was cheating on me." "My husband's a sailor. He had an affair, so I jumped ship. I've been happy ever since."

Constant fighting and **emotional abuse** were the number three and four reasons people gave for their divorces:

"There was no food and no money, and we fought constantly. We seemed to argue constantly." "We fought nonstop during my first year of marriage." "What did we do most of the time? We fought, fought, fought."

Falling out of love was the one clearly romantic cause among the five main reasons that Americans leave their spouses. But it ranked fifth.

"My husband and I lived different lives and we had completely different values." "No more love was involved." "I was unsure if I still loved my spouse. That told me I didn't. I was brave enough to leave the marriage."

Where do people think divorces will most likely occur in the future? There was a huge variance from region to region around the country. New Englanders were the ones most dissatisfied with their current marriages. Forty-seven percent of them said that they will probably be divorced in the next five years.

✶ BY REGION: LIKELY TO BE DIVORCED IN THE NEXT FIVE YEARS
(National Average: 25%)

(For a map of America's regions, See Part I.)

Region	Percentage	Region	Percentage
New England	47%	Metropolis	27%
Granary	29	New South	16
Pac Rim	28	Old Dixie	15
Rust Belt	28	Marlboro Country	10
L.A.–Mex	27		

★ | **DIVORCE: THE TOP TEN REASONS BEHIND DIVORCES IN AMERICA**

Americans gave these reasons why they got divorced. They were allowed to give more than one reason.

Cause	Percentage Who Agree
Communication problems	64%
Spouse's infidelity	58
Constant fighting	58
Emotional abuse	52
Falling out of love	49
Unsatisfactory sex	45
Spouse didn't make enough money	31
Physical abuse	28
Falling in love with somebody else	22
Boredom	22

12

★ ★ ★ ★ ★

Infidelity: It's Rampant in All Nine Regions

For years, Tom Wolfe wouldn't write fiction (not until *The Bonfire of the Vanities*). Wolfe said that what was reported in the news every day was more interesting and shocking than anything he could make up.

Here is some current nonfiction on the subject of infidelity.

THE NATIONAL STATISTICS FOR ADULTERY

Almost one-third of all married Americans (31 percent) have had or are now having an affair. This isn't a number from Hollywood or New York City. It's the national average for adultery.

The affairs aren't one-night stands either. American affairs last, on the average, almost a year. That shows more staying power than do many American marriages.

The end is not in sight. Only a minority of those who are cheating (28 percent) have any plans to end their current affairs soon.

So move over, Jackie Collins. Forget about *Hollywood Wives* and *Holly-*

wood Husbands. Here's what is *really* happening in Boston and Birmingham and in any other U.S. city or town you name.

Today, the majority of Americans (62 percent) think that there's nothing morally wrong with the affairs they're having. Once again, we hear the killer rationalization that "everybody else does it too."

That's what adulterers honestly believe. The great majority of men and women having affairs firmly believe that other married men and women do the same. That "everybody" does not, however, include the offended marital partner: Less than one-fourth of adulterers of either sex think that their own spouses are paying them back in the same sexual currency.

Most of us (78 percent) also believe that we're cheating at a greater rate than Americans did as recently as twenty years ago. Whether we are or not, our numbers far exceed anything ever before reported in this country.

A SCARLET LETTER IN MODERN-DAY WISCONSIN

"I remember having this picture of people all across the state sitting across the breakfast table from their spouses, opening the newspaper, and suddenly spilling coffee all over themselves."
> —The attorney for Donna E. Carroll, arrested in 1989 on a charge of adultery, recalls the day the story of her arrest was on page one of Wisconsin's newspapers.

EVEN BIRDS DO IT

"Ah, romance. Can any sight be as sweet as a pair of mallard ducks gliding gracefully across a pond, male by female, seemingly inseparable? Or better yet, two cygnet swans, which, as biologists have always told us, remain coupled for life, their necks and fates lovingly intertwined?

"Coupled for life, with just a bit of adultery, cuckoldry, and gang rape on the side.

"Alas for sentiment and the greeting card industry, biologists lately have discovered that, in the animal kingdom, there is almost no such thing as monogamy. In a burst of new studies that are destroying many of the most deeply cherished notions about animal mating habits, researchers report that even among species assumed to have faithful tendencies and to need a strong pair bond to rear their young, infidelity is rampant. . . .

" 'This is an extremely hot topic,' said Paul W. Sherman, a biologist at Cornell University in Ithaca, New York. 'You can hardly pick up a current issue of an ornithology journal without seeing a report of another supposedly monogamous species that isn't. It's causing a revolution in bird biology.' "
> —*New York Times*, August 21, 1990

THE ANATOMY OF AN AMERICAN AFFAIR

The typical American affair is not likely to become anything more than that. Only a small proportion of those currently dallying (17 percent of men and 10 percent of women) say that they intend to leave their spouses. Even fewer (9 percent of men and 6 percent of women) plan to marry their current lovers.

"Playing around" is a relatively new field in which American women have come a long way, without as yet having achieved full parity. About one married woman in four cheats vs. one man in three. Men still initiate most liaisons, but the number of affairs started by women—almost one in three—is higher than it has ever been.

We saw interesting differences in the way men and women view their extramarital adventures.

★ | **BY REGION: INFIDELITY IN THOUGHT AND DEED**

(For a map of America's regions, see Part I.)

EVER CONSIDERED HAVING AN AFFAIR (National Average: 49%)

Region	Percentage Who Have Considered Having an Affair
Granary	54%
Metropolis	54
L.A.–Mex	53
New South	52
Old Dixie	50
Pac Rim	45
New England	44
Rust Belt	43
Marlboro Country	35

EVER HAD AN AFFAIR (National Average: 31%)

Region	Percentage Who Have Had an Affair
New England	39%
Metropolis	33
Old Dixie	33
Granary	31
New South	31
L.A.–Mex	31
Pac Rim	30
Rust Belt	29
Marlboro Country	21

The majority of women say that they like their lovers better than they like their husbands.

Men say the reverse: They like their wives better.

Affairs are more habit-forming for men: Two-thirds of men vs. 40 percent of women have had more than one affair.

Love doesn't have much to do with it for either sex, but even less for men: Two-thirds of men say that they don't love their current lovers vs. 57 percent of women.

"Just a sexual fling" is said more often by men than by women. That may be because most men adulterers say that they still love their spouses.

Those who are likeliest to be cheating include gays and bisexuals, blacks, liberals, and the poor.

Despite their Puritan heritage, Protestants get around more than Jewish people and especially more than Catholics. As a rule, those who cheat least say that they did it "for love." Catholics cheat least.

There is still *some* guilt around. Gays and bisexuals are much more likely to say that they feel guilty about cheating. Blacks feel more guilt

---

★ | PROFILE: AN ADULTERER

Woman, in her early forties, white, married with teenage children, lives in the Pac Rim region:

She has had four affairs during her marriage: with a friend of her husband, two neighbors, and a veterinarian.

She attributes her current affair, which has lasted two years, to a form of blackmail: "He reminded me of how many favors he had done for me over the years. One thing led to another."

She says that she prefers her husband to all of her lovers, none of whom she ever loved. She doesn't expect to divorce her husband, nor does she plan to end her current affair.

She says that she is an Open Book to most people, but she has concealed her bisexual desires from her husband. She has had sex a few times with a woman, and her favorite fantasy is "making love with a woman, using oral sex, kissing from head to toe, kissing her breasts, and using my tongue on her whole body till orgasm."

She says her husband is very secretive. He never includes her in financial decisions. "He is too private an individual. I also found out that he cheated on me many times. He has denied it and refuses to talk about it. These are the things I hate about him, but I also love him very much."

Her father "made sexual advances . . . trying to kiss me on the lips." She resents her mother for not protecting her but, instead, "turning her back on the things she did not want to see."

than whites, the poor a lot more than the rich. Protestants feel it more than Catholics, but Jews outdo them both in self-reproach.

It doesn't take much to get most of us to consider infidelity. Sixty-seven percent of us are tempted at least once a week, and some—more men than women—say that they're tempted more often.

There is, we found, a significant regional difference between thought and deed when it comes to adultery.

People in some areas of the country specialize in thinking about it, others in the deed.

When it comes to the extramarital deed itself, New England has the highest rate.

American affairs are usually casual in their origins. Most of those involved in an affair say that it started by accident rather than by design.

Most often, it was a chance encounter, and frequently it happened in a bar. "A businesswoman at my bar made a pass, so I took her up on it,"

ADULTERY: HOW IT HAPPENS

How	Percentage of Respondents
Casual meeting/met at a bar	28%
Just happened/accident	12
Growing friendship	10
Introduced by friend	7
Sexual attraction	7
Pursued by eventual lover	7
Old flame	3
Mid-life crisis	2

. . . AND WITH WHOM

Whom	Percentage of Respondents
Friend	24%
Co-worker	23
Old flame	21
Stranger	20
Friend of spouse	15
Prostitute	9
Boss	7

said a retired Air Force man in his late thirties. "I met this good-looking man at a bar when I was out with 'the girls' "—a woman from the East Coast in her fifties, who has had two affairs but is sure of her husband's fidelity.

What about the third parties—the cheatees? They may be the last to know for sure, but they sense that something's wrong. Only 16 percent of our respondents said they were *sure* that their spouses were cheating on them. On the other hand, 35 percent *suspected* their mates of straying.

That's just four percentage points more than the actual figure of 31 percent—a very good guess!

In other words, if you think that there might be a problem, there definitely might be a problem. Adultery in contemporary America is as likely to occur in Manhattan, Kansas, as it is in Manhattan, New York.

13

The End of Childhood in America

Many, many parents told us they fear that their children are growing up too fast. They said that they feel it instinctively, very strongly, and everywhere they look. However, many of those parents did nothing to stop it from happening.

American children do not have the idealized youth of earlier generations—whether that even existed in fact or not, we believed that it did. The growing-up years of eleven to sixteen have changed to the point that it's accurate to speak of the end of childhood.

DO YOU *REALLY* KNOW WHERE YOUR CHILDREN ARE?

Most parents don't know where their children are.

Our children are starting sex earlier—far earlier—than in any previous generations. One in five kids now lose their virginity before the age of 13. (Because of the difficulty in interviewing children, we feel that that number is probably conservative.)

100

Whatever happened to childhood? "I'll tell you," a Los Angeles elementary school teacher recently said in the *Los Angeles Times*. "Children are skipping it."

★ | **THE VIRGIN VANISHES**

How many people answered "Yes" to the question, "Were you a virgin on your wedding night?"

Age Group	Percentage Who Say "Yes"
★ Baby boomers (25–44)	29%
Baby boomers' parents (45–64)	42
Baby boomers' grandparents (65 and older)	41

Children are actually launching another sexual revolution—one that is much deeper and more profound than the sexual liberation movement of the 1960s and 1970s.

The first revolution, led by the baby boom generation, ended the double standard as it applied to virginity at marriage. In previous generations, many more women than men came to the altar as virgins. The baby boomers changed that in the 1960s. Not men, though, whose behavior was remarkably consistent. (One-fourth of the baby boomer men were virgins at marriage—exactly the figure reported by their fathers and grandfathers.) But for women, the change was dramatic—from 57 percent virgins at marriage in the preceding generations to only 34 percent among baby boomer women. The baby boomers effectively disconnected sex from marriage. They made sex outside matrimony acceptable to a growing majority.

But the baby boomers did not start sex earlier than their parents. They just married later.

In both generations, and in those before them, most people were adults when they made love for the first time.

Not this generation. Among the "baby busters" (now eighteen to twenty-four years old), almost two-thirds (61 percent) revealed that they had lost their virginity by the age of sixteen.

More than one in five lost it at age thirteen or younger.

Those numbers show a break with the past. Some might say that the numbers show a revolution.

In the decades of the 1920s through the 1950s, the number of people who started sex by the age of sixteen averaged only 24 percent. For thirteen-year-olds, it never exceeded 5 percent. That's less than one-fourth of today's rate.

WHAT IS SEX LIKE FOR A TWELVE-YEAR-OLD?

The baby busters who started having sex at age twelve or thirteen didn't do it for love. Only 10 percent of them give love as their reason for having sex.

Nor do they have sex for the pleasure of sex itself. No irresistible physical urge is driving them on.

★ | **PROFILE: FIFTEEN, GOING ON THIRTY-FIVE**

Girl, fifteen years old, lives in New England, annual family income $90,000:

★

She lost her virginity at age thirteen and has gone to bed with six other boys since them. She says that she doesn't see the big deal about sex. She can't see herself married, but she likes kids and would like a baby.

She considers herself more adult than either of her parents. She considers her parents "nice enough, but dopy."

She says that she's seen an awful lot already and can't imagine that life has a lot of hidden mysteries to be revealed later on.

Her friends say that she's beautiful. She gets good grades in school. She has spending money and has been promised a car when she's old enough.

★

She has thought about suicide but says that's normal—so have most of her friends.

Pleasure rates down there with love as a motive for early sex among twelve-, thirteen-, and fourteen-year-olds.

Overwhelmingly, the reason teenagers give for starting sex so early is the powerful force of peer pressure—peer pressure without any effective counterforce from many parents or from schools.

Consider this scene at a California high school: It's Friday afternoon, and the students are leaving a class in "social living." The teacher's parting words are, "Have a great weekend. Be safe. Buckle up. Just say, 'No' . . . and if you can't say 'No,' then use a condom!"

The teacher explains her philosophy: "I try to give support to everyone's value system. So I say, 'If you're a virgin, fine. If you're sexually active, fine. If you're gay, fine.' "

That's just California, some people will say. But for more than a decade now, California has been setting our cultural pace.

There is a beautiful girl named Danielle at a birthday party. She's wearing tight pants, a designer blouse, and dangling earrings. She is gyrating to rock music. "I want your sex, I want your body!" suggests a song from George Michael.

✴ | WHO IS SEXUALLY PRECOCIOUS?

Overall, 14 percent of Americans lost their virginity by the age of thirteen. But it happens more within some groups than within others.

Group	Percentage
Males	22%
Females	7
Blacks	35
Whites	12
Ages 18–24	25
Ages 25–44	13
Ages 45–64	10
Ages 65 and older	5
Income less than $10,000	19
Income more than $45,000	14

Danielle wins first prize in the contest for "sexiest performance." Danielle is in the fourth grade.

Adults are selling sex to children like Danielle in order to sell them on cosmetics, clothes, and music tapes. Most girls aged nine to eleven use nail polish, hair conditioner, and deodorant, and in the next two years, they'll add perfume, lipstick, blush, and eyeshadow. By age thirteen, many girls are spending over $250 a year on adult cosmetics.

Early sex is only the most poignant aspect of the end of childhood.

After a long detour, during which a goal of our society was to comfortably lengthen childhood, we seem to be returning to the practices of Victorian, or even medieval times, when children were hurried into the work force as early as possible.

Do you remember any of the following images from your own childhood?

"There was a time when youngsters rushed home from school to Mom, wolfed down milk and cookies, then raced outside for what seemed like endless devotion to throwing balls, skating, riding bicycles, and playing

---

★ **DATING IN THE FOURTH GRADE**

"Dr. Antoinette Saunders, a clinical psychologist in Evanston, Illinois, knew a nine-year-old boy who told his parents that other children in his fourth-grade class were dating and that he was very confused about what he should do.

★ " 'He was torn between being a kid, dressing up in a G.I. Joe costume on weekends, and having to pair off with a girl to fit in,' she said. 'There is so much pressure to grow up fast. Dating can be a stressful situation for kids. It has everything to do with how kids think they should be acting, not what they really want to do.'

"Betsey Davis has already set her limits. 'I will not let my daughter date,' she said. 'She is tall and leggy, with hair to the waist, and has a very active suitor who sent her a long-stemmed rose for Valentine's Day. The boy just turned ten. My

★ daughter is eight years old.' "
—*New York Times*, May 3, 1990

★ **EARLY SEX AND KINKY SEX**

| | Percentage | |
Activity	Population Average	Sexually Precocious*
Anal sex	37%	60%
Sex in a public place	31	57
Sex with sexual devices	31	53
Interracial sex	29	62
Watching others have sex	28	62
Sex with multiple partners	20	60
Sex with a prostitute	17	41
Sex with someone of the same sex	14	36
Swapped spouses	13	43
Sex with violence	9	26
Sadomasochistic sex	8	25
Sex with urination	7	21
Incest	6	19
Sex with a child	4	14
Sex with defecation	3	10

*Lost one's virginity at the age of thirteen or younger

hopscotch. It was unstructured play, the kind that psychologists believe fosters intelligence and creativity. And in retrospect, the middle decades of the twentieth century appear to have been the golden age of childhood."

Few of our children will experience anything like that.

Instead, we heard story after story like this one: A nine-year-old asks his working mother: "Mom, what's the difference between a regular condom and a French tickler?"

There is something about the loss of childhood that reaches deeper than any specifics. There's a feeling of emptiness, a sense that something is missing, but that it doesn't even have a name yet.

Bret Easton Ellis, twenty years old at the time, conveyed the feeling in his best-selling novel *Less Than Zero*. Here, two former teenage lovers look back in angst:

"What do you care about? What makes you happy?"
"Nothing. Nothing makes me happy. I like nothing," I tell her.
"Did you ever care about me, Clay?"
I don't say anything, look back at the menu.
"Did you ever care about me?" she asks again.
"I don't want to care. If I care about things, it'll just be worse, it'll just be another thing to worry about. It's less painful if I don't care."
"I cared about you for a little while."
I don't say anything.

14

What Men Really Think About Women; What Women Really Think About Men; and the Real Truth About Both

The sexual revolution of the 1960s and 1970s has left American men and women of the 1990s in separate worlds. They stare at each other with indifference or, often, hostility.

What do men honestly think about women?

In our interviews, it was evident that the majority of men still see women through the lens of traditional stereotypes. Women are seen as pussycats, or at least as cats; their biology is their destiny; they nest; they shop; they cry for no discernible reason. Norman Mailer once said, "You don't know anything about a woman until you meet her in court." Sylvester Stallone has been quoted as saying, "I have all the reason in the world to be a misogynist."

What do women really think about men?

Women see men as predators; bullies; boys; the primary provider; even as meal tickets. Most women express some fear and concern about the physical (or violent) side of American men.

Women still wonder, and worry whether a man can be sensitive and not be a wimp. This is consistent in both rural and urban parts of the country.

WOMEN ARE THE MORAL SEX

One thing isn't confusing anymore, not to women, nor to men:

Women are the more moral sex. That's one of the only propositions that the two sexes absolutely agree on.

Women lie less, steal less, fight less, do drugs less, are less often drunk on the road or on the job. Women are more responsible, more loyal at work, more faithful in their relationships. Women make better citizens, better team players.

Yet it's still a man's world. Half of the men and two-thirds of the women said that men have the easier life. (On this issue, as on many others, blacks parted company with whites. Most blacks believe that women have it easier.)

Forty-five percent of men say that their best friend is a woman.

Only 37 percent of women find their best friend in a man.

Marriage has been an institution that supposedly protected women from the consequences of male tomcatting. As you might expect, women do not fully share the view that marriage is on the rocks. That marriage "till death do us part" is outdated, that the institution itself will be obsolete by the year 2000, that most marriages will end in divorce: These are all opinions held by some women but by many more men.

On the other hand, the proposition that "parents have an obligation to stick it out in a bad marriage for the sake of the children" got the agreement of 41 percent of the men vs. only 26 percent of women.

WHAT WOMEN SAY ABOUT MEN IN THE POWDER ROOM

We thought that it would be an interesting experience—for men especially—to hear what some contemporary women really say about men when they talk among themselves.

The scene is an office building in a metropolitan city. The participants are all professional women, college graduates, with an interviewer.

WOMEN: THE HONEST SEX

PEOPLE WHO BELIEVE THAT IT'S ALL RIGHT TO LIE . . .

Why	Men	Women
To protect oneself	63%	52%
To avoid personal embarrassment	56	48
To keep one's job	56	35
To make oneself look better	28	19
To gain a small amount of money	25	15
To get even with someone	16	8

PEOPLE WHO HAVE STOLEN . . .

From Whom	Men	Women
Store	27%	17%
Parent	25	11
Stranger	20	6
Friend	19	7
Boss	15	8
Lover	13	8
Neighbor	13	3
Co-worker	10	1
Client/customer	10	3
Work subordinate	9	2
Child	7	3

WOMEN: BETTER WORKERS

Activity	Percentage	
	Men	Women
Participated in unethical practices at work	23%	14%
Took office supplies	38	32
Lied to boss	27	18
Lied to co-worker	19	13
Was drunk at work	15	4
Used drugs at work	12	4
Left work early without telling anyone	19	11
Had an affair with a co-worker	13	6
Stole valuable company property	6	1
Goofed off at work	35	30

WOMEN: THE LESS LARCENOUS SEX

Activity	Percentage	
	Men	Women
Cheated on a test or exam	43%	27%
Lied on a job application	40	26
Borrowed money without repaying it	30	16
Cheated on income taxes	29	21
Exaggerated on an insurance claim	27	14

Activity	Percentage	
	Men	Women
Shoplifted	26	16
Used an expense account to entertain a personal friend	19	5
Took a kickback or bribe	15	4

WOMEN: THE MORE DILIGENT AND PERSEVERING SEX

Belief	Percentage Who Agree	
	Men	Women
The way to get ahead is by politics, not by hard work	50%	42%
I expect to compromise values to get ahead	32	20
The only way to get ahead is to cheat	19	8

WOMEN: THE LESS ADDICTED SEX

Addiction	Percentage Who Are Addicts	
	Men	Women
Alcohol	32%	18%
Illegal drugs	26	19
Gambling	12	5

WOMEN: THE GENTLER SEX

People Who Have Ever . . .	Percentage	
	Men	Women
Gotten into a shoving match	61%	30%
Challenged someone to a fight	56	26
Gotten into a fistfight	54	20
Hit someone with an object	35	29
Sent someone to the hospital	19	5
Threatened someone with a knife	13	6
Threatened someone with a gun	13	5
Cut someone with a knife	10	3
Shot someone with a gun	8	2

Weapon Carried	Percentage	
	Men	Women
Knife	15%	4%
Gun	12	4

WOMEN: THE MORE SUSPICIOUS SEX

Activity	Percentage	
	Men	Women
Searched spouse/lover's wallet/purse	34%	56%
Secretly gone through spouse/lover's mail	28	46
Checked up on spouse/lover's whereabouts	40	45

Activity	Percentage	
	Men	Women
Searched child's room	28	43
Questioned spouse/lover's friend	35	42
Secretly gone through child's mail	23	38
Listened in on spouse/lover's phone call	19	28
Listened in on child's phone call	17	25
Secretly followed spouse/lover	22	22
Secretly followed child	18	16

ANIMALS WE ASSOCIATE WITH THE OPPOSITE SEX

ANIMALS MEN ASSOCIATE WITH WOMEN:

Animal	Percentage of Men
Cat/kitten	41%
Dove/bird	6
Deer/doe	4
Lamb/sheep	4

ANIMALS WOMEN ASSOCIATE WITH MEN:

Animal	Percentage of Women
Dog	23%
Predator (lion/tiger)	21
Gorilla/ape/monkey	8
Donkey/horse	5
Wolf/fox	5
Bull/ox	4
Weasel/snake/rat	4

INTERVIEWER: Please write down the first thing that pops into your mind when I say "women."

WOMAN #1: "Superior Race." I just think that women are basically better than men. I think that they're more interesting, more emotional, insightful, have a lot more depth to their character, are more open, are more caring, are not that limited. They're emotionally more open than men, and interesting and loving and smart.

WOMAN #2: "Great and interesting." If I think about people I know and the people I care about, and the people I think are special, I tend to have many more women than men who fall in that category.

WOMAN #3: "Understanding." When you talk to a woman, she listens, and she hears what you're saying. Whereas, when you talk to a man, it's just what's there. You don't get any more. I think men do not have the feel for the way our needs change. With a man, it's like being in a time warp. It's as if he's saying, "Wait a second. You just got me bent all out of shape because you were crying." And the woman says, "Oh, that's past. I've gotten rid of that." The man goes off and has a heart attack, and the woman has totally gotten it out of her system.

★ | **WHAT WOMEN SAID ABOUT MEN ACROSS AMERICA**

Things that women said to us about men:

- "How dumb they are . . . they're not brain surgeons, not even the brain surgeons."—a young saleswoman from the East, never married, lives with her lover.
- "I think Mick Jagger had a rare insight: 'Men are beasts of burden!' "—a married woman from the East Coast.
- "The best man, that rare keeper, gives good check."—an East Coast woman, married twice.
- "I think men have a great sense of fairness. If you keep everything on that basis, they respond very well."—a psychologist from the West Coast, married.
- "How well can he perform?"—an educator from the South, in her fifties, never married, lives alone.
- "That they can be lying assholes."—a nineteen-year-old laborer from the Midwest, never married, lives with a roommate.
- "Give me nice biceps. I'll jump on that any old time."—a West Coast widow in her late twenties.
- "Perverts, by and large. They are all after one thing."—a married woman from the Midwest, in her early twenties.
- "Need a mother to tell them what to do. Sometimes, I like that too."—a West Coast budget assistant, in her thirties, married.
- "How they are in bed and the size of their dick. For talk and companionship, I've got lots of girl friends."—a married woman from the Southwest, in her late thirties.

The talk eventually turns to the real role of men in their lives:

WOMAN #1: I don't have any friends that are men. I mean, it's about sex for me. I feel very fulfilled in all other areas. I really think I've built up a life where I can almost function without a man.

WOMAN #2: I feel like I'm not validated without a male partner in some ways because I was brought up that way. You know, very strict, Catholic. But there's the other side of me that is completely validated without them. I do matter in this world without a man.

WOMAN #3: That's an issue that a lot of women feel the same about. I think you just said it. A lot of women in their late thirties who are not paired off with somebody have that exact feeling, like they feel very good and accepted in other aspects of their lives.

WOMAN #2: But they're not validated.

WOMAN #3: Yeah.

WOMAN #4: It's like you have to take care of men. It's not two strong, equal individuals who are coming together at the same place. I feel like the woman is more integrated and stronger and has been through more. And then here comes this guy who has needs and speaks with a forked tongue and acts like he's liberated. But he's not liberated, and he doesn't really want you to be independent either. It's . . . I don't know. I just think they're not as evolved.

WOMAN #5: I think the only successful relationship I've ever had was with the first man who wasn't threatened by my career. And that's the man I married.

WOMAN #6: Think about the times when you're away from home on business. I find that men are completely helpless when we're not around, and you see another side of them all of a sudden. He's like a very strong, macho man, who can do everything. And you go away on business for two weeks, and they fall apart. It's like they don't know what to do with themselves.

WOMAN #5: You know what else is interesting? When spouses die, almost within the year, men will hook up with somebody and remarry. I think they need a partner no matter. I think women are much stronger and don't need to jump into the next relationship.

WOMAN #6: Actually, a lot of widows become amazingly euphoric, even if they loved their husbands.

WOMAN #4: See, I wish sometimes men could just act like women.

WOMAN #1: The whole idea that the man is supposed to be the strong person in the relationship and the provider, we're criticizing all of these things about guys—and then, on the other hand, when they're not that way, it's sometimes perceived as a lack of strength.

INTERVIEWER: That's a point. A lot of women I know break up relationships if the guy's wimpy.

WOMAN #2: So we're saying, "Why can't they be more like women?" Women are understanding, women are emotional, women are vulnerable. Then, when we find men like that, we don't want them.

WOMAN #4: I used to have male friends, but they're never as good as female friends.

WOMAN #2: All my male friends are gay.

INTERVIEWER: When I say the word "men," write down a word.

★ | **"MOMMY"**

★ "I love intelligent women. I love to go home and talk to women who want to talk about politics or birth control or, God forbid, baseball. Forty years ago, my mother didn't go to college, she didn't go to high school. She was one-dimensional, raised the kids. And one night, the night my father died, I stayed up until five o'clock in the morning with our two friends, drinking beer with my mother, which I had never done in my life. And I found out that here was a woman that was incredibly talented, an incredible brain. I thought of her as Mommy. Then, all of a sudden, she's telling me she listens to Itzhak Perlman and all these things when my father wasn't in the house, because he felt threatened that she liked something he didn't understand completely. And I think that was very typical of that generation. And what a damn shame. And it's too bad we don't spend more

★ time understanding who women really are, and they don't do the same really finding out about who we are."

—Man, in his late forties, white, father of two, college graduate, business executive.

WOMAN #1: "Boys." I don't think of women as girls. But I do think about all these little boys running around. They're big children, and incredibly needy.

WOMAN #2: Very needy.

WOMAN #3: "Self-centered." When you meet a guy for the first time, it's amazing how little they ask about you. You'll sit and you'll spend two hours having dinner with them, and they'll tell you everything about themselves. And they won't ask a thing about you. I don't think the key to a man's heart is through his stomach. It's through your ears. Because I think that men will fall in love with you if you're a great listener.

INTERVIEWER: What would you say is the greatest area of conflict between men and women?

WOMAN #4: Control. Who's going to sit in the driver's seat.

WHAT MEN SAY ABOUT WOMEN IN THE LOCKER ROOM

The participants now are all professional men, friends, drinking buddies. Here are the kinds of things men say about women over a few beers.

INTERVIEWER: Just tell us the first word that pops into your mind when you think of women.

MAN #1: "Erratic." My mother was erratic. My sister's erratic. I think one of my downfalls is unpredictable and erratic women.

MAN #2: "Voluptuous."

MAN #3: "Ambivalence." Women have two personalities—modern-day women anyway, the ones I deal with. They have this necessity to prove themselves in the business world, or to prove themselves the equivalent of men on a lot of levels. But underneath it all, there's this driving desire to make a nest. So part of them is constantly fighting. You can meet the most qualified woman intellectual, and underneath that, when you scratch the surface, you find someone who wants to build a nest.

MAN #2: I think when a girl is coming up the street, men look at her tits. Nobody looks at their minds. And that's all they say: "What's the matter? Why don't you look at my mind?"

INTERVIEWER: Which sex has a better fix on the needs and priorities of the other sex?

MAN #4: Women are more perceptive about life in general. Plus they spend much more time thinking about certain things than men do. Men are in business doing this or that. Women have more time to do it. They spend half their life doing that.

MAN #3: People came in and made women aware that they had brains and there was something better in life than just raising children. Well, that may be right and may be wrong. But it still goes against everything in nature.

INTERVIEWER: What do you think are the ground rules today?

MAN #3: I believe there are new ground rules. I don't quite understand them, and that's why I stay without a relationship.

MAN #2: I think there are instincts deep down with women.

MAN #1: They're unbelievable.

MAN #2: Women think—no, they *know*—we're providers.

MAN #4: The need to have a baby is unbelievable. They have no control over it. Something inside them is saying, "You got to reproduce. You have only so many more years. Reproduce! Reproduce!"

MAN #1: Women are captives of their bodies.

MAN #2: Of course they are.

MAN #4: If I get married again (I got married twice) I wouldn't marry a woman that works. I don't want to get involved with women that work. It interferes with life. I like to play a lot of golf on weekends. And if you can't hack that, don't get involved with me. That's my opinion.

INTERVIEWER: Do you think it was better the way it was, when women stayed home?

MAN #2: Women aren't dedicated to business the way men are. They come in at nine, they work until five. In my opinion, I think that, basically, they're looking for a husband. They're not going to go and support the family—at least not if they have a choice.

MAN #1: I feel a tremendous amount of confusion in my generation.

MAN #3: I think women have more difficulty dealing with men's idiosyncrasies than men do dealing with women's idiosyncrasies.

INTERVIEWER: Are women more honest than men?

MAN #5: I think they are, yeah. They think they're more honest, see. They blurt out stuff that we can't understand.

MAN #4: One pussy hair has got more power than a church full of saints. I wish I could say it in Italian. That's women's power and their strength. That's the only way they can control the male.

ONE CONCLUSION

A bad attitude exists right now between American men and women. This attitude is contributing to the problem between the sexes.

A majority of men believe that women expect men to understand women's emerging needs but that women aren't willing to reciprocate with men. They don't try to understand the problems of being a man. Men feel that the situation has become completely unfair and weighted against them. "Men die earlier," one man said, "and I don't think women have stopped to think about why that's so. Most men have the pressure of responsibility thrust on them, and it goes from cradle to early grave."

This bitterness is widespread, and it runs deep among the men we talked to. It surfaced in interview after interview, when men began to talk about what they *really* think and believe. It's creating a counter-trend toward the past: the old T&A (tits and ass) syndrome is returning. It also has the potential to spawn a revolution among men—a men's movement.

Women have changed during the past couple of decades; that is clear from our interviews. Women are more confident about themselves, more outspoken, much more involved in the work force. The previous documentation of this accurately matches our data: Women's superiority in morals and ethics, while suspected by some, is overwhelming.

The rhetoric of the women's movement, however, seems to have helped to create caricatures of men, stereotyping, and bigotry. At least, it came up often in our interviews. As necessary as this stereotyping may have been as a catalyst to change, it has now become another obstacle to reconciliation between the sexes.

But stereotyping is happening with both sexes right now. Most men and women seem to have little experience that results in an understanding of the opposite sex. Their views are largely shaped by myth and word of mouth from friends. Listening to American men talk about women is like listening to them talk about world politics. They know very little, but

★ | WHAT MEN ACROSS AMERICA SAID ABOUT WOMEN

★
- "They're greedy, lesser people."—a designer from the West Coast, in his thirties, never married.
- "Men are superior to women. The proof is everywhere. Who runs the world?"—an East Coast man, in his late thirties, married.
- "They act and dress too much like men, yet they never pick up the check."—an East Coast filmmaker, in his twenties, never married, lives alone.
- "Sure, women forced the issue, but at least men made an effort to understand what their needs are. Women stereotype men and make no effort to understand."—an East Coast salesman, married.

★
- "They're a huge pain in the ass but nice to have around."—an unemployed man from the East, in his thirties, divorced.
- "They are only good for one thing; two, if she can cook."—a Southern cop, in his forties, married.
- "That they are sorry bitches and only good for one thing."—a Midwestern welder, twenties, never married.

★
- "I know why my wife likes modern dance. I love it that she does. She's made no effort to understand why I love the things I do."—a lawyer from the South.
- "They're cows. You walk into any K-Mart in the country, you'll see nothing but cows, I guarantee it."—a gas station owner from the Midwest.

★
- "This won't sound very enlightened of me, but it's accurate. When a man marries a woman, two things happen: One, the woman changes; two, she tries to change you. Almost no man will disagree with that."—a medical doctor on the West Coast.

what they know, they're adamant about. Women often talk about men with the same lack of real understanding. And they're inflexible about their views as well. In interview after interview, both sexes were entrenched in their stereotypes and prejudices about the other sex.

Almost half of all men think of women as kittens.

Almost half of all women think of men as dogs or predators.

VI

AMERICAN VIOLENCE

15

The Most Violent Country
in the World

In the story by Robert Louis Stevenson, the respectable Dr. Jekyll invented Mr. Hyde so that he could act on his darkest desires without being blamed for the results. In the end, the evil self triumphed over the good self, and Hyde took over completely.

The spirit of Edward Hyde, the evil half of Dr. Jekyll, seems to live in almost half of us. That's how many people across the nation confessed that violent desires obsessively force their way into their minds.

It's not all fantasy. One in four Americans say that they've acted on their violent impulses. An equal number think that they'll do so at some time in the future.

We asked just what the Hyde within us has on his—or her—mind.

JEKYLL AND HYDE IN THE 1990s

- "Beating people up for no reason, to destroy them," said a man who considers himself a good and ethical person. Violence is part of his

119

real life as well as his fantasy life. He's been involved in dozens of fights, cut someone with a knife, sent someone to the hospital. His father beat his mother and ignored his children. This man's darkest secret is that when he was ten, he molested a little girl.

VIOLENCE: THE UNITED STATES VS. THE WORLD

We compared violence in this country to what has been documented around the world.

- Young men do most of our killing and dying. The homicide rate among young American males is twenty times that of Western Europe and forty times the Japanese rate.
- A study in the *New England Journal of Medicine* makes the point that young males in Harlem are less likely to survive to the age of forty than are their counterparts in Bangladesh.
- The United States has twenty times the number of rapes reported in Japan, England, and Spain.
- Guns were used in three-fourths of the killings in America vs. one-fourth of those in other industrialized nations.

THE MODERN KILLING FIELDS:
HOMICIDE RATES IN ELEVEN DEVELOPED COUNTRIES

Country	Homicide Rate Per 100,000 People	
	Men	Women
United States	13.9	4.1
Czechoslovakia	3.4	1.3
Hungary	3.1	1.9
Canada	2.7	1.4
Australia	2.4	1.5
Italy	2.4	0.6
Spain	2.0	0.4
France	1.5	0.9
West Germany	1.1	1.1
Japan	0.9	0.6
United Kingdom	0.8	0.6

- "I can imagine mutilating and torturing people," said a divorced woman from the East. Sexually active since the age of fourteen, she has had over forty partners. She used to have a drug problem, and her life has been affected by other people's addictions to drugs and alcohol. She has used force on others and suffered it in return. She owns a handgun and carries it.

- "Shoving a broomstick up a guy's ass." —a woman from the East Coast.
- "Killing someone for fun. Just blasting somebody," said a single man in his late thirties, who once shot someone and still owns a rifle.
- "Driving into an oncoming car," said a grade-school teacher from the East Coast in her early thirties. She had her first experience of sex at age thirty.
- And these imagined vendettas: "Urge to pulverize annoying, difficult, obnoxious people." "I feel like shooting my ex-boyfriend." "Slugging the harbor master I dislike." "Beating up on people just because I don't like them." "I'd like to kill or hurt the girl my husband was having an affair with." "I get so ticked off at my boss, I'd like to belt her." "To thrash people who hurt my friends."

Sometimes sex gets into our thoughts of violence:

- "I think of women being raped and children being molested." —a divorced woman in her twenties from the Northwest, a regular churchgoer.
- "To strike a child over and over. To fuck my best friend's brother." —a single woman from the Southwest, who carries a gun and has felt a strong desire to kill.
- "Killing someone and getting away with it. Raping someone." —a young crew leader in the Northwest, who owns but does not carry a gun.
- "Telling my boss to go to hell. Fucking some particularly good-looking guys." —a woman clerk from the West Coast, in her thirties,

---

TRUE CONFESSIONS

What follows is a chilling excerpt from a murder confession made by Thomas Lyndon, Jr., of Rocky Point, Long Island, on how he planned to kill a sleeping St. James, Long Island, woman, whom he had found during the course of a robbery. He admitted that he aimed a four-inch hunting knife blade directly at Lea Greene's throat and "dug it in a little deeper" after she awoke and attempted to struggle. He says that after the woman stopped moving, "I counted her heartbeats out of curiosity to see how long it'd take her to die . . . I knew exactly what I was doing . . . I knew it was against the law . . . I felt pretty powerful—invincible, sort of, you know?"

Lyndon even remembered how many times her heart beat after he severed her jugular vein, 74 times.

a Buddhist, who has used force, has wanted to kill, and carries a handgun.

- "Blow up the world and start all over again. I'd like to kill everybody." —a single man in his late fifties, a virgin, who used to have a drinking problem. He has never wanted to kill any individual human being—just *all* of us.

★ | **PROFILE: A 1990s MR. HYDE**

Man, in his early thirties, white, Catholic, lives alone, postgraduate degree:

Violent desires course through his mind: "Killing someone, a random stranger, someone physically near me, my mother or brother, a person who dated a former girl friend of mine. . . ."

So far, he has never acted on these impulses. "Punching out" people is the most violent action he's taken. "Punching out a few windows."

Pornography is central to his life. He knows that he is "relying too heavily on pornography for sexual satisfaction" and that this is affecting his potential relationships with women.

He is an extreme loner who says that no one, including himself, completely knows him. He has contemplated suicide on several occasions. He lists the reasons:

"I felt nobody liked me, and I couldn't blame them."
"I felt I had no future that I care to pursue."
"I felt a failure, even at being a bad guy."
"I thought I'd never have another girl after a relationship ended."

MEDIA VIOLENCE

Our role models have also grown more violent.

There was a time when movie heroes needed a cause before committing acts of violence and mayhem. In the 1990s, because we don't believe in our institutions anymore, our movie heroes today are loners, even misanthropes. They are cynical about everything; self-interested, almost never involved in a team effort; capable of expressing themselves with weapons only. Sylvester Stallone, Clint Eastwood, Arnold Schwartzenegger, and Mel Gibson often play the parts of loners or men who have only a single buddy in the world.

★ | **BY REGION: LOOKING FOR MR. GOODBAR**

(For a map of America's regions, see Part I.)

REGULAR VIOLENT FANTASIES (National Average: 42%)

Region	Percentage	Region	Percentage
Granary	53%	Marlboro Country	39%
Metropolis	45	Old Dixie	37
New South	44	Rust Belt	37
Pac Rim	42	New England	26
L.A.–Mex	42		

THE ELECTRONIC BABY-SITTER

Finally, there is the sheer volume of violent messages that reaches our children, mostly on TV.

Children's programming now averages twenty-five violent acts per hour. That rate is up 50 percent from that of the early 1980s. Much of the violence is depicted by the three major networks as humorous.

Ninety-five percent of all children's TV cartoons have violent themes.

ACT (Action for Children's Television) is a nonprofit group that promotes diversity and the lessening of violence on children's shows. The president of ACT commented, "When you think of Saturday morning as the network affiliates' service to kids, then you know why we are the laughingstock of countries that care about their kids."

★ | **SUMMER MOVIE BODY COUNT**

Here is an approximate number (body counts are always approximate) from some American movies—our entertainment. Many of these are considered children's films.

Film	Body Count
Public Enemy (1931)	8
Death Wish (1974)	8
Die Hard (1988)	18
Robocop (1987)	32
Rambo II (1985)	62
Total Recall (1990)	74
Rambo III (1988)	106

Among the kids' shows honored by ACT are *CNN Newsroom, Nickelodeon's Quiz Show,* and *Make the Grade.* Many of the shows not honored are aimed specifically at young boys. They include *G.I. Joe* and *He-Man.*

Commentary about violent children's shows comes from the Center for Psychological Studies in the Nuclear Age at Harvard Medical School:

"The heroes are usually white, blond, and blue-eyed; the enemies are non-Caucasians with thick accents. . . . [The cartoons] teach white children that the world is a frightening place, that they must not trust anyone who looks different or has an accent, and that there is no such thing as peaceful compromise. . . . For nonwhite children, the underlying message seems to be that darker skin and accents are undesirable, even evil."

Whether we are adults or children, the sheer volume of the violence that we witness is numbing. We wonder where it's all going to stop, but it keeps escalating. And this urge toward violent action is creating real epidemics in America, epidemics of violence.

16

Child Abuse: An American Epidemic

It has often been reported that when abused children grow up, they become troubled adults, likely to pass the suffering on to their own children. This is another of America's secrets, perhaps our saddest.

THE TRUTH ABOUT CHILD ABUSE

One in six adults across America were physically abused in childhood.

Almost as many, one in seven, confess that they were victims of sexual abuse as children. Four in ten Americans know someone who was abused as a child. And bear in mind that most of the people abused as children tell no one.

The great majority of those who were sexually abused (three-fourths) are women.

People are very secretive about their childhood traumas. How secretive?

Almost half said that nobody knows about what happened to them. They had never told anyone of the experience before they told us.

ADULT CHILD-ABUSE VICTIMS AND NONABUSED ADULTS

Issue	Percentage of Nonabused Adults	Percentage of Sexual-abuse Victims
Things you intentionally haven't told your spouse/lover	40%	61%
Believe you are likely to be divorced in five years	25	38
Currently divorced/separated	16	23
Married more than once	17	25
Have used drugs	41	55
Have contemplated suicide	32	50
Have suffered date rape (women)	20	33

The nightmares and troubles of child-abuse victims do not end when they grow up. Women who were sexually abused as children are much more likely to suffer date rape as adults. Child-abuse victims are also more prone to a wide range of ills, ranging from drugs to marital problems.

Some people were willing to tell us about the ways in which they'd been abused as children:

- "My stepfather sexually abused me. I told my mother. She didn't believe me, so I left home at age twelve."—a woman from the South, bisexual, never married.
- "I was raped by my uncle's friend."—a Southern man, who has had problems controlling his drinking and has considered suicide. He said that he expects to wind up in hell when he dies.
- "My aunt used a vibrator on me, and then I used it on her one night when I was sixteen."—a West Coast woman in her fifties.
- "Raped at age eleven."—a twenty-eight-year-old bartender, bisexual, who had six sex partners in the last year.
- "I was raped by a baby-sitter."—a Northwestern woman, divorced, with a drug problem. She has an active sex life (seven partners in the last year and forty overall) and has contemplated suicide more than once. She expects to go to heaven.
- This testimony from other childhood sex victims: "Raped by a grown man." "When I was no older than eight, a neighboring boy raped me." "Sexual abuse by a kindly old neighbor." "Beatings and rape." "Beaten, raped by my father and uncle."
- Others were molested as children: "My grandfather molested me." "My cousin attempted to molest me." "Molestation by my mother."

"My grandfather fondled me." "I was molested by my uncle when I was seven."

- There are victims of physical abuse: "Hit with an electric cord, then my mother took a knife to me." "My father used to burn me with a poker." "The old razor strap every weekend when my father was drinking." "My father broke the hallway mirror over me. Said I was using it to sex myself up before school." "Beat up by my father when he was drunk." "Beatings by two stepfathers." "Beaten with belt." "Constantly beat every day." "My dad would beat up my mother and me when he was drunk." "Beatings for no reason." "Hit by broom or kicked." "Father punched me through our storm door."

Many of us still don't understand what child abuse really is or realize that we may have been victims ourselves. We project the thought that it doesn't happen to people like us, that it's the exception rather than the national plague that it clearly has become. Some of us believe that it is the stuff of talk shows, not everyday reality.

But the hard fact is that one in every six Americans was seriously abused as a child.

This unfortunately is an American reality.

17

Date Rape

Child abuse isn't the only epidemic across this country. There is another serious problem—date rape—and the numbers are huge.

HOW REAL IS DATE RAPE?

Twenty percent of the women we spoke to told us that they had been raped on a date.

Projected nationally, that figure means that as many as 19 million women have been the victim of date rape in America.

Another 4 percent told us that they were not sure if they had been raped—a figure that, in its own way, is just as startling.

Here is the problem in a nutshell: Most women aren't surprised by these statistics. Men, on the other hand, typically say, "None of my friends ever raped anybody. Neither have I. I don't buy your numbers."

But our numbers are *real*. If anything, they're *low*.

HOW DOES DATE RAPE OCCUR?

Date rape is something that the young do to each other—the average age of both victim and rapist is eighteen.

The fears and peer pressures of youth help explain why so few cases are reported. More than half of the victims of date rape tell no one, and only one in twenty goes to the police—figures that help explain why the epidemic goes untreated.

According to Dr. David Elkind, author of *Hurried Child,* only about 5 percent of the victims of date rape ever report the offense.

This estimate finds corroboration in a sociological study conducted on University of Massachusetts undergraduate coeds, which found that only 3 percent of date-rape victims report the attack.

A victim explains her silence: She was a college freshman, just short of eighteen years old, living in a coed dorm. He was a junior, an athlete at least twice her size. He raped her in his room after a dorm party. She said nothing about it because "Who would believe me? He was a really good player. No one would have believed me if I said anything. All I would have received was even more shame and guilt. Believe me, I didn't ask for it."

Another victim, this one in high school at the time, said that she told no one because "I felt I couldn't go to my parents—the police were out—and my friends would quickly disown me for having one of our own thrown in jail."

Too often, the women don't fight back as much as they are able to. Later, they think that they should have.

This date-rape victim was also a college freshman. She recalls her feelings after it happened: "I *felt* raped, but I didn't realize I had *been* raped. I felt I had been an unwilling participant and that the woman was always guilty until it had been proved that she had been knocked unconscious, or doped and mutilated, before being raped. It didn't occur to me that it was okay to hurt him, to kick him in the balls, or punch him in the eye. Good girls didn't do that."

Here is another female victim: Like the 4 percent in our survey who didn't know if they'd been raped, she could not call what had happened by its proper name: "I never told anyone I was raped. I would not have thought that was what it was. It was 'unwilling sex.' I just didn't want to, and he did. Today, at twenty-nine, I know it was rape."

Women often blame themselves for going out with the wrong man and letting themselves be maneuvered into the wrong situation. To this, some rape counselors have the reply, "Poor judgment is not a rapable offense."

DATE-RAPIST PROFILE

Most date-rapists are not Jack-the-Ripper types. This woman was raped twice, both times by men she knew: "Both of the guys were Joe Average types. Both were intelligent and articulate. Nothing about their exterior packaging spelled 'rapist.' "

Joe Average isn't usually a rapist, but most date rapists appear to be average. However, they usually start having sex a little younger than most men, drink more, and have violence in their family background. They believe in a macho mythology in which sex is a form of combat. They believe that women who resist really want to be raped.

Date rape is even more epidemic among gay men. Thirty-seven percent of our homosexual or bisexual respondents said that they had been raped by men they knew.

STOPPING AN EPIDEMIC

The problem is twofold. First, victims need to come forward and report cases of rape, whether they occur on a date or not. Right now, less than 3 percent of date rapes are reported. Secondly, men must understand that date rape happens a lot. It is a serious situation all across America. Like child abuse, it is an epidemic.

19

Guns: No Roses

Talk-show host Johnny Carson put it this way in a comedy monologue: "You can get more with a kind word and a gun than you can with a kind word alone." A lot of us in this country agree with Johnny Carson.

Every seventh person you pass on the street in America is carrying a weapon either on their person or in their car.

Americans are the most heavily armed people on earth.

Americans use their weapons, too. "People have a tendency to use the amount of power at their disposal," New York City's Police Chief, Lee P. Brown, said after three children had been accidentally killed by gunfire in a single week. "All too often, we find the power at their disposal turns out to be a gun." His Chief of Detectives, Joseph R. Borelli, added, "There is an overall attitude out there that life is cheap. Years ago you would get into a shouting match. Now, they pull out a gun and shoot."

HANDGUNS

One-third of the people we talked to have handguns. Almost as many have rifles or shotguns. More than one in ten have semiautomatics, the weapon of choice of *Miami Vice*–style drug dealers. Most people have these weapons illegally.

DON'T LEAVE HOME WITHOUT IT

When they go out, 26 million Americans carry a weapon with them. Usually it's a knife or a handgun; sometimes it's both.

Most Americans approve of violence as a problem-solver. About two-thirds think that the use of physical force is often justified. About six in ten say that they have used physical violence against another person. Less than half of them regret their action.

BY REGION: WHERE THE GUNS ARE

(For a map of America's regions, see Part I.)

PEOPLE WHO CARRY WEAPONS: (National Average: 14%)

Region	Percentage	Region	Percentage
Marlboro Country	25%	Pac Rim	12%
New South	18	Metropolis	11
Granary	17	Old Dixie	10
L.A.–Mex	16	New England	9
Rust Belt	14		

OWNING A HANDGUN AROUND THE WORLD

In the United States, handgun purchasers must be twenty-one years old, rifle buyers eighteen. They must swear on a form that they're not felons or mentally incompetent. In most states, the policy is cash and carry.

Japan. Civilian possession of handguns is banned, with exemptions for sport shooters and athletic competitions.

Great Britain. A police permit, required for handgun possession, is rarely granted, except to sport shooters. Carrying handguns is barred.

A great many of us (29 percent) report being physically injured by another person. The aggressor is most often a stranger. If not, it's most likely to be a spouse.

We like our violence even when it's only movie make-believe. Most polls show Americans saying that there's too much violence and sex in the movies. Not true. In our interviews, people admitted that they like plenty of both in their escapist fare.

SUICIDE IN AMERICA

Many more Americans kill themselves each year than the official suicide statistics indicate.

Almost half of our respondents (47 percent) knew someone, usually a person close to them, who committed suicide. We believe that the official total of about 30,000 a year far understates the true extent of suicide in America. One-third of our respondents say that they have seriously contemplated suicide, and most say that they've considered it on more than one occasion.

SUICIDE: WHO THINKS ABOUT IT

WHO'S MOST LIKELY TO CONTEMPLATE SUICIDE?

Group	Percentage
Women	34%
Men	28
Homosexuals/bisexuals	37
Heterosexuals	32
Whites	32
Blacks	16
Ages 18–24	41
Ages 25–44	32
Ages 45–64	25
Ages 65 and older	17
Noncollege	32
College graduate	28
Liberal	37
Conservative	30
Income less than $10,000	38
Income more than $45,000	27

BY REGION: WHERE THE POTENTIAL SUICIDES LIVE

(For a map of America's regions, see Part I.)

THOUGHT ABOUT COMMITTING SUICIDE (National Average: 32%)

Region	Percentage
Pac Rim	40%
Granary	36
L.A.–Mex	34
Metropolis	32
New England	31
Rust Belt	31
Old Dixie	28
New South	27
Marlboro Country	25

OFFICIALLY REPORTED SUICIDES

Sex	Total
Men	24,226
Women	6,678

MODES OF SUICIDE

Mode	Percentage Men	Women
Firearms	64%	40%
Poisons	15	38
Hanging	16	13
Other	5	9

Facts on Suicide

People think about suicide more in the Pac Rim, and women are more likely than men to consider it. But more men than women do, in fact, kill themselves.

Older people talk about it less but do it more. Their attempts are far more often successful than those of younger people.

Many of America's unreported suicides are elderly people and among those, many are helped out of life by their children or friends.

People draw a definite distinction between suicide in general and suicide among the elderly. Suicide, most said, is immoral, and more than half believe that it is a sin punishable by God because, by its nature, it cannot be punished in this life. Yet a majority of people also said that they believe the elderly have the moral right to end their lives. Almost half said that if asked, they would help their terminally ill parents commit suicide.

19

The Violence of AIDS

On any night of any week, several hundred thousand of us unwittingly make love with someone who thinks they have AIDS. We don't know, because our lovers haven't told us.

Among Americans who are certain that they have AIDS, more than one in three would *not* tell their spouses or lovers—that is, would not give the other person a chance to decide whether to risk AIDS for the sake of making love.

The sudden appearance of AIDS has forced many of us to confront moral choices in our sexual behavior. All too many Americans are willing—and will even *say* that they are willing—to risk infecting their lovers with the disease that is killing them. They seem to value their own sexual pleasure more than they value their lovers' lives.

Extrapolating from our numbers, some 2.2 million Americans are reasonably certain that they have AIDS.

That's just the beginning. Another 7 million people see themselves as being at very high risk for AIDS. The majority of those people, both those who are certain and those who believe that they are at high risk, are heterosexuals.

The rate of AIDS is far higher among gays. So is sex itself. Gays are twice as likely as heterosexuals are to have sex more than once a day. They are four times as likely to have had 100 or more lovers (11 percent) than are heterosexuals (3 percent); and they are four times as likely to have had ten or more lovers in the past year (16 percent) than are heterosexuals (4 percent).

Fear produces many responses. Some gays abstain from sex, but almost half (42 percent) admit that they still take no precautions against AIDS.

Many of those who continue a promiscuous lifestyle may believe, like the people we see in paintings carousing during the Black Death, that it's too late for them anyway. Possibly with good reason: One in four of our gay respondents believe that they've had sex with someone who they think was infected.

AIDS: RISKING THE LIVES OF YOUR LOVERS

Question	Percentage of Population	Percentage of Homosexuals and Bisexuals
"Did you ever have sex with someone knowing that he/she may be infected with AIDS?"	4.1%	18%
"Did you put any person at risk of catching the AIDS virus in the past ten years?"	6.6	18

HOW WE REALLY FEEL ABOUT AIDS

- Forty percent of Americans believe that AIDS sufferers deserve it.
- Sixty-four percent believe that AIDS tests should be mandatory for all Americans aged eighteen and older.
- Fifty-two percent believe that the names of AIDS carriers should be made public to protect the general population.
- Sixty-seven percent believe that known AIDS carriers who don't practice safe sex should be thrown into jail.

BY REGION: WHERE GAY AND LESBIAN AMERICANS LIVE

(For a map of America's regions, see Part I.)

ENGAGED IN SEX WITH SOMEONE OF THE SAME SEX (National Average: 14%)

Region	Percentage	Region	Percentage
Pac Rim	22%	Marlboro Country	12%
L.A.–Mex	18	Metropolis	11
Old Dixie	15	New South	11
Rust Belt	14	New England	8
Granary	13		

★ | **PROFILE: GAY FATHER**

Man, in his thirties, white, divorced, lives in the Granary region:

★

He's been tested for AIDS, he takes precautions, and he says that he has altered his sexual behavior. Yet he also says that he never has asked about AIDS before sex and that he's had sex with men he knew might be infected.

Sex is at the center of his life. His most serious lies have been told about sex: to his parents, that he was straight; to his wife, that he was faithful to her; to his gay lover, that he was faithful to him.

He claims to have fully accepted his homosexuality but he is full of contradictions about it. He says that he is willing to "die for my right to be the person I have grown to be"—but he hasn't told his closest friend that he is gay.

★

He says that he loves his children and would die for them. He has never told his children that he doesn't want to be a father.

His current sexual relationship is relatively stable. He has had four lovers in the past year. But over the years—and he's only in his early thirties—he says that he has had more than 300 sex partners. His favorite fantasy is having sex with strangers and, obviously, he has acted on it.

★

Promiscuity, along with his onetime heavy drinking, have combined to get him into "embarrassing and dangerous sexual situations."

VII

WORK

20

The Best and Worst
Occupations in America:
What America Really
Thinks About Your Job

The original master of the ten-second sound bite might have been Mark Twain. Twain said, "It could probably be shown by facts and figures that there is no distinctly native American criminal class except Congress."

Based on what we heard, his opinion was pretty close to current thought.

We asked people across the country to rank 73 occupations for their honesty and integrity, including the job of Congressman. Then we asked them to give each occupation a letter grade from A (for Excellent) to F (for Failure).

Consider the jobs rated highest. They aren't high-income jobs. They aren't the classic prestige occupations either. In fact, look at where the "prestige" occupations rate with most people:

★ AMERICANS GRADE PROFESSIONS FOR HONESTY AND INTEGRITY

Profession	Grade Point Average (out of 4.00)	Grade
Fireman	3.07	B
Paramedic	3.02	
★ Farmer	3.00	
Pharmacist	2.91	
Grade school teacher	2.88	
Mailman	2.82	
Catholic priest	2.81	
Housekeeper	2.80	
★ Baby-sitter	2.79	
College professor	2.77	
Airline pilot	2.76	
Rabbi	2.73	B−
Scientist	2.72	
★ Chef/cook	2.68	
Flight attendant	2.68	
Dentist	2.66	
Engineer	2.66	
Accountant	2.65	
Protestant minister	2.64	
Medical doctor	2.64	
★ Judge	2.51	
Banker	2.49	
Social worker	2.49	
Waitress	2.48	
Garbage collector	2.47	
Policeman	2.47	
★ Supreme Court Justice	2.46	
U.S. Attorney General	2.43	
Novelist	2.42	
Book publisher	2.40	
Funeral director	2.39	
U.S. military officer	2.39	
Plumber	2.37	
★ Construction worker	2.35	
President of U.S.	2.35	
TV news anchor	2.32	
Airline executive	2.31	
TV reporter	2.30	C+
★ Bartender	2.28	
Newspaper reporter	2.18	
IRS official	2.17	
Sex therapist	2.17	
College athlete	2.16	
Building contractor	2.14	

Profession	Grade Point Average (out of 4.00)	Grade
TV talk-show host	2.13	
Advertising executive	2.11	
Cab driver	2.08	
Professional athlete	2.07	
Movie critic	2.06	
Stockbroker	2.04	
U.S. Senator	2.03	
Prison guard	2.02	
Investment broker	2.00	
Motion picture star	2.00	
Soap opera star	2.00	
Lawyer	1.97	C
Oil company executive	1.94	
TV network executive	1.94	
Real estate agent	1.92	
Wall Street executive	1.92	
Labor union leader	1.89	
Insurance salesman	1.76	
Rock and roll star	1.72	C−
Car salesman	1.59	
Congressman	1.58	
Local politician	1.52	
Street peddler	1.45	
Prostitute	1.24	
TV evangelist	1.19	
Organized crime boss	0.99	D
Drug dealer	0.61	F

TOP TWENTY: THE OCCUPATIONS AMERICANS MOST ADMIRE

1. Fireman
2. Paramedic
3. Farmer
4. Pharmacist
5. Grade school teacher
6. Mailman
7. Catholic priest
8. Housekeeper
9. Baby-sitter
10. College professor
11. Airline pilot
12. Rabbi
13. Scientist
14. Chef/cook

15. Flight attendant
16. Dentist
17. Engineer
18. Accountant
19. Protestant minister
★   20. Medical doctor

BOTTOM TWENTY: AMERICA'S SLEAZIEST WAYS TO MAKE A LIVING

1. Drug dealer
2. Organized crime boss
3. TV evangelist
★   4. Prostitute
5. Street peddler
6. Local politician
7. Congressman
8. Car salesman
9. Rock and roll star
★   10. Insurance salesman
11. Labor union leader
12. Wall Street executive
13. Real estate agent
14. TV network executive
15. Oil company executive
16. Lawyer
★   17. Soap opera star
18. Motion picture star
19. Investment broker
20. Prison guard

★   **PARAMEDICS AND FIREMEN IN THE JUNGLE**

New York newspapers reported on a new problem for their city. Motorists were regularly refusing to let ambulances and fire trucks get through traffic to reach their emergencies.

★   In one case, a double-parked pickup truck refused to move for an ambulance. The paramedics finally had to take the dying woman out of their ambulance and wheel her down the street to the hospital. "She could have died right there," one of the paramedics said. "The two guys in the truck didn't care."

Not one of the traditional greed occupations appears in the top ten nor, for that matter, in the top twenty—no lawyers, no stockbrokers.

In fact, lawyers and Wall Street brokers are in the twenty occupations that Americans rated lowest for honesty and integrity. So are TV network executives.

Down at the bottom of the moral sink, we find TV evangelists. They barely nose out drug dealers and crime bosses. But all of them fail to match the moral standards of prostitutes.

Americans rated members of Congress and local politicians as well. Being honest, rather than merely showing their rancor, people ranked Congressmen among the seven least-moral professions in America.

Make what you will of some of our findings:

- Agents for the Internal Revenue Service are tied with sex therapists for thirty-fourth place.
- Catholic priests rated higher than rabbis, who rated higher than Protestant ministers.
- Oil company executives were tied with TV network executives—with a grade of C.
- U.S. Senators rank below building contractors and TV talk-show hosts.
- TV and newspaper reporters were below waitresses and policemen.

Finally, the President's honesty and integrity was rated in twenty-eighth place. That's a notch below the average plumber—and we're not talking about the Watergate variety of plumber either.

That's the overall picture on how Americans really feel about occupations. Now let's look closely at how corporate America is faring.

AMERICA'S CORPORATIONS: THE MOST ETHICAL

These were the names most frequently mentioned when we asked our respondents which they thought was America's most ethical corporation:

★

    IBM
    Sears
    Johnson & Johnson
    Ford
    Chrysler
★   Walt Disney
    AT&T
    McDonald's

21

Modern American Business: Greed at the Top

Much has been written on the loss of world market share by American businesses and why we can't seem to compete the way we used to. According to thousands of workers and bosses, one very important and underestimated reason is clear: The perceived low ethics of management is a major cause of our problems in the business world.

Greed in American management is out of control. Never have so many taken so much, right off the top.

★ | **THE TROUBLE WITH BUSINESS TODAY**

"The trouble with the rat race is that even if you win, you're still a rat."
—Lily Tomlin

When we asked about their business ethics, American executives pointed a shaking finger of guilt—at themselves.

They know that they're doing wrong. The managers' views of their own actions, their own morality, is even lower than the one their workers have of them.

In addition, modern American managers show little loyalty to their companies, to their workers, or to the public that buys those products.

American workers reply with absenteeism, petty theft, indifference, and a generally poor performance on the job.

The American business system often creaks and grinds to a halt, and it's the Japanese or Europeans who get the next order. The syndrome has gotten worse every year of the past decade. Let's start at the top and see why.

THE BOSSES

Former NCAA championship basketball coach Al McGuire once observed, "I think the world is run by *C* students." McGuire has pretty high standards, and he keeps being disappointed by the leaders he meets.

The consensus is that our business executives are enriching themselves beyond any kind of acceptable level, while impoverishing America.

As a direct consequence, there is no loyalty in many companies. The very idea is scorned: "You want loyalty? Hire a cocker spaniel!" one of our interviewees told us.

Other thoughts we heard:

- "GM isn't what it was, and they were never all that great to us."—a GM worker.
- "There used to be a sense of family around here—not since the buyout."—a General Foods manager.
- "You want to be loyal, you want to belong to something better than

---

✦ **AMERICA AND JAPAN: THE DIFFERENCE IN EXECUTIVE PRIVILEGE**

"The income gap between American and Japanese business executives is astounding. . . . There is no way that [a Japanese executive] could expect to equal the luxuries enjoyed by American executives. Mr. Matushita, probably the wealthiest man in Japan, when traveling abroad with his secretary, uses regular commercial flights. Having a private plane is simply out of his realm of consideration.

"[An American] corporate chairman with whom I am acquainted complained that he has no use for all the money he receives. His company is doing well, and his income is in the multi-million-dollar-a-year range. His children are all grown, and he and his wife already have vacation villas, a yacht, and a private airplane. He said they just have no way to spend any more money on themselves."

—Akio Morita, Chairman of Sony Corporation

yourself, but they make it impossible."—a Shearson Lehman executive.
- "Everybody is for themselves now. Nobody's for First National Bank."—a First National Bank of Chicago employee.
- "They lie to us every single day."—a former Wendy's employee.
- "James Brown is in jail while Ross Johnson walks free. Something's wrong here."—a former RJR worker, a black woman.

Several workers told us about the unethical things they'd actually seen executives do. The misdeeds most often witnessed: intimidating and threatening employees; violating job safety standards; discriminating against blacks, Hispanics, or Asians; discriminating against women; sexually harassing women; overt criminal actions; making products that endanger lives.

On Wall Street and in Hollywood, two places where the sharks are especially thick, there's a common feeling that the younger carnivores are even more voracious than their elders.

"It's like *Lord of the Flies,* with the yuppies in middle management," said one businessman we spoke to. "It's emotionally draining just to come to work in the morning."

The movie business was never particularly noted for its business morality. But Jere Henshaw, a producer who's been around for thirty years, told the *Los Angeles Times* that the new breed of Hollywood executive has turned the personal trust that used to govern deal-making into a joke.

"The older hands get depressed," Henshaw said. "There's a lack of morality among the younger set. Lying has become a way of life. What's frustrating is that I don't see any measurable reward for honesty or forthrightness."

★ | **A NEW YORK EXECUTIVE TELLS HOW THE SYSTEM WORKS**

"Not every but too many senior executives have their price. That's why there are these exorbitant salaries at the top of a lot of companies. We won't admit it, not even to ourselves, but we've been bought. If we deliver profits, at almost any cost, then we get ludicrous bonuses—millions of dollars.

"This is how the system works and it's repeated in most companies: Money is put on the table for top executives, especially the top dog. A lot of money. Enough money to make it impossible for the executive not to do what is 'necessary.' Let's say it's $15 million if the numbers are delivered—nothing if they aren't. That kind of money can cause someone to rationalize a lot of decisions, especially when it comes to cutbacks. In a sense, the big money packages create a conflict of interest for the executive: 'Do I do the right thing by my people? Or by the bottom line (including my bottom line)?' An incredible amount of rationalizing goes on. 'This is for the good of the company; it has nothing to do with my $15 million.' That kind of interior dialogue.

"I'd like to say I could rationalize what I've done in terms of people in my own company. I can't. I was bought."

> —Man in his mid-forties, white, married, earns above $500,000 a year plus bonuses.

★ | **BOSSES VS. WORKERS**

Question	Percentage of Managers Who Agree	Percentage of Workers Who Agree
Who works harder?		
Workers	43%	60%
Managers	31	18
Who is more ethical?		
Workers	37	37
Managers	13	19
Who is more greedy?		
Workers	10	15
Managers	61	53
Who is more trustworthy?		
Workers	32	40
Managers	14	14
Who takes credit for another's work?		
Workers	18	23
Managers	50	58
Who cares most?		
Workers	26	41
Managers	29	24

BOSSES' ETHICS: THE WORKERS' REPORT

Thirty percent of American workers say that their employer engages in at least one of the following kinds of unethical activities:

Activity	Percentage of All Workers
Intimidates and threatens employees regularly	15%
Violates job safety standards	11
Discriminates against blacks, Hispanics, or Asians	11
Discriminates against women or sexually harasses them	11
Engages in criminal activities	5
Makes products that endanger human lives	4

BUSINESS ETHICS IN THE NEWS

Business stories like these are so commonplace today that they often don't even make the front page of our newspapers:

"The General Electric Company, which was convicted in a jury trial of overcharging the Army for a battlefield computer system, agreed yesterday to pay one of the largest fines ever assessed for defrauding the Defense Department. G. E. will pay $16.1 million in criminal and civil penalties.

"The Northrop Corporation agreed to pay $17 million for falsifying test data on components of the Cruise missile and the Harrier jet. The largest military fraud settlement was reached in 1988, when the Sundstrand Corporation paid $115 million for overbilling the Government for military hardware."
—New York Times, July 27, 1990

T E S T **III** ★　★　★　★　★　★　★　★　★　★

How do you actually compare with other bosses? To find out, take the test below. Answer the yes-or-no questions. Then see where you stand, compared with bosses across the country. (By the way, you don't have to be the Chairman of IBM to take this test. If you have a couple of people reporting to you at work, that's enough.)

ARE YOU AN ETHICAL BOSS?

1. The federal government evaluates hiring and promotion decisions. Do you believe that they would find that you've discriminated against anyone because of race, creed, sex, or sexual preference?
2. Have you ever lied to those who work for you in the interest of the company?
3. Do you generally keep your employees in the dark about your decisions, even decisions that affect them personally?
4. Do you think that you have the right to fire employees without explanation or due process?
5. Two equally qualified people apply for the same job. Would you be inclined to hire the one who's better looking?
6. Would you feel uncomfortable hiring someone who weighs 300 pounds?
7. Do you think that it's your right to take full credit for the work of your subordinates?
8. Do you think that you have the right to ask your subordinates to break the law in the interest of the company, so long as no one is hurt and there's no risk that anyone will be caught?
9. A major client, or your own boss, asks you to get him a date with a woman who works for you. Would you do it?
10. A subordinate refuses to work on a major company project because he believes that the client's selling arms to third-world countries is immoral. Would you force him to do the work anyway?
11. Have you ever asked an employee to do personal errands for you?
12. Have you ever made promises to employees that you knew you could not keep?
13. Do you believe that it's your responsibility to protect the interests of those who work for you, even at the company's expense?
14. An employee gets access to vital information about one of your competitors, but the means he used were illegal. Would you use the information?

15. If your own boss asked you to bug the offices of your subordinates, would you do it?
16. Do you have people who spy on their fellow employees for you?
17. Your boss asks you to fire one of your people to make room for a relative. Would you do it?
18. Do you deliberately pit your subordinates against each other in order to get more out of them?
19. Do you ask subordinates to do your dirty work?
20. Would you fire or transfer someone just because he or she rubbed you the wrong way?
21. Would you fire someone because you thought that he or she posed a threat to your position?
22. X is your best worker. X's secretary comes to you to complain about X's constant sexual advances. Would you fire X?
23. Do you use threats to invoke fear among those who work for you?
24. Have you ever asked a subordinate to do something for you for which he or she could have been fired?
25. Y is down with the flu and feeling terrible. But Y is the only worker who can handle the assignment. Would you insist that Y keep on working?
26. Have you ever blamed a subordinate for something that was your own fault in order to save your job or to avoid embarrassment?
27. Dumping hazardous waste into the ocean is the only way to save your company and the jobs of its employees. It's also illegal. Would you ask a subordinate to help you do it?
28. Either you take a 10 percent cut in pay or you will have to lay off one member of your staff. Would you take the pay cut?
29. Do you accept responsibility for the acts of your subordinates even when they reflect poorly on you?

Give yourself one point for any of the following questions marked Yes: 13, 22, 28, 29.

Give yourself one point for any of the following questions marked No: 1, 2, 3, 4, 5, 6, 7, 8, 9, 10, 11, 12, 14, 15, 16, 17, 18, 19, 20, 21, 23, 24, 25, 26, 27.

Add up your score: _____.

NATIONAL RESULTS

Score	Percentage of the Population Who Scored		Rating
	Above You	Below You	
23–29	5%	95%	Ethical boss
22	10	90	
21	20	80	
20	30	70	
19	50	50	
18	60	40	
17	70	30	
15–16	80	20	
3–14	90	10	
0– 2	95	5	Unethical boss

22

American Workers Get to Tell the Truth

Here is the quid pro quo in the American workplace today.

American workers are as disloyal to their jobs as their bosses and companies are perceived to be disloyal to them.

Over their life span, the average American worker will spend 76,900 hours on the job. That's a big part of their lives—by far the biggest waking activity.

But to hear person after person tell it, Americans make poor use of those working hours.

Q: How many people work in your office?
A: About half of them.

That old joke isn't far from the truth in the 1990s.

THE TRUTH AS WORKERS SEE IT

The so-called Protestant ethic is long gone from today's American workplace.

Workers around America frankly admit that they spend more than 20 percent (7 hours a week) of their time at work totally goofing off. That amounts to a four-day work week across the nation.

Almost half of us admit to chronic malingering, calling in sick when we are not sick, and doing it regularly.

One in six Americans regularly drink or use drugs on the job.

Only one in four give work their best effort; only one in four work to realize their human potential rather than merely to keep the wolf from the door.

But then, why should we? After all, half of us genuinely believe that you get ahead not through hard work but through politics and cheating.

About one in four expect to compromise their personal beliefs in order to get ahead on their current job.

CAN'T GET NO SATISFACTION

Only one in ten say that they are satisfied with their jobs. Only three in ten Americans say that they are loyal to their companies.

★ **BY REGION: MODERN AMERICAN WORKERS**

(For a map of America's regions, see Part I.)

VERY SATISFIED WITH JOB (National Average: 20%)

Region	Percentage	Region	Percentage
Marlboro Country	35%	New South	19%
Old Dixie	33	Pac Rim	18
Granary	25	Metropolis	17
L.A.–Mex	22	New England	12
Rust Belt	19		

PUT TOTAL EFFORT INTO JOB (National Average: 45%)

Region	Percentage	Region	Percentage
Marlboro Country	65%	Metropolis	43%
New South	52	Old Dixie	40
Granary	48	Pac Rim	39
L.A.–Mex	46	New England	27
Rust Belt	45		

Americans are happiest and do their best at work in Marlboro Country. New England is at the opposite pole: Its residents admit that they are the least satisfied with their jobs and the least willing to give work their total effort.

Few of us are willing to put the public interest above our pocketbooks. Most people told us that they would quit their jobs before they would take a pay cut so that the following problems could be fixed:

- Discrimination against women, blacks, or Hispanics
- Production of products that endanger human lives
- Prevention of employee layoffs without sufficient notice
- Pollution of the environment

The reason they would quit is key: Americans don't trust the managers who make these financial decisions, supposedly for the common good. They believe that managers make decisions with only their own interests at heart. Why then should workers be the ones to sacrifice?

Many American workers say that they cannot trust their co-workers (43 percent) or subordinates (38 percent) in the current business environment. Maybe it isn't surprising when you listen to what people say about their jobs.

WHAT PEOPLE SAY ABOUT THEIR WORK

In the boardroom. "We were all millionaires, yet we thought it compassionate that we took no bonus at a time when thousands were being fired in our company. That's how out of touch we'd become."

Stealing. "Our night manager steals from the company nightly. We call him The Burglar." "Everybody steals supplies out of the warehouse." "Co-workers take money out of the cash register." "My boss has taken money and given merchandise away."

Lying. "Bosses often ask someone to say a job's done when we haven't even started." "There's constant lying to clients about completion of quotas." "We all lie to clients, every one of us, to every one of our clients."

Cheating. "Cheating people out of pay." "Leaving work without finishing the job." "Shameful misuse of company materials and company time." "Cover-ups for jobs not done." "Falsification of a lot of sign-in sheets which get billed."

Sex. "Secret meetings in the closet. . . . My girl friend is boffing the boss during lunch." "Employees loving each other in the store after we close." "Sexual harassment by our gay boss. He hits on the men in his department."

★ | **THE TOP FIVE OFFICE CRIMES**

| 1. Taking office supplies and equipment
| 2. Lying to a boss or co-worker
| 3. Stealing company funds
| 4. Affair with a boss or co-worker
★ | 5. Taking credit for work not done

Doctoring documents. "Falsified reports." "Shady accounting." "Signing someone else's name." "Altering of many official records." "Signing by other people, not the applicant." "Using false company names." "People falsifying forms for leave." "Incorrect work turned in to fill quotas. Everything we do down in South America!"

OFFICE CRIME

It's not surprising that we see so many locked doors or that companies are turning to what's called "integrity testing" in rising numbers. These are tests (not including lie detectors, which are banned by law) that are given to job applicants in an effort to screen out would-be thieves. This kind of business testing is growing by more than 20 percent a year.

Super D Drugs, a chain in the Southeast, turned to integrity testing after a dramatic rise in what they called "shrinkage." The company's Vice-President for Loss Prevention said that the tests are already saving $400,000 in stolen goods.

The New South, where Super D Drugs operates, ranks second only to Metropolis in its rate of unethical employees. Old Dixie is close behind those two.

You don't have to bolt the door quite so tightly in New England and Marlboro Country, where workers' ethics are strongest.

The Case for Hiring Women Over Men

Our current ethics at work are low, but they'd be a lot lower were it not for the great number of women who've entered the work force in recent years.

When we compared the answers given by the two sexes, we confirmed that women in this country simply behave more ethically than men.

On every question we probed, American women in the workplace held to a higher moral standard than men did.

✶ | **BOSSES AND WORKERS: THE GROWING GAP**

"Between 1981 and 1989, the net worth of the Forbes 400 richest Americans nearly tripled. Corporate executives also made strides in this area. In 1980, corporate Chief Executive Officers made roughly forty times the income of average factory workers. By 1989, CEOs were making 93 times as much."
—Kevin P. Phillips, author of *The Politics of Rich and Poor: Wealth and the American Electorate in the Reagan Aftermath*

Most women—but only a minority of men—are loyal to the company that pays them (60 percent vs. 46 percent).

Less than half as many women as men believe that the only way to get ahead is to cheat, and not as many believe in politics rather than work as the way to success.

In addition, women are much less willing to compromise their values to get ahead and somewhat more willing to quit as a matter of principle if they learn that their company is engaging in illegal activities.

Look for the Man

In their on-the-job behavior, women are less likely, usually by pretty big margins, to take office supplies home, to malinger, to lie to bosses and co-workers, to leave early, or to goof off. Management is much less likely to find a woman drunk at work or on drugs. If valuable company property is stolen, the thief will be a man six times in seven.

At work, as in private life, women set a higher standard of ethics.

AMERICA'S BUSINESS FUTURE

High-school seniors proved even more cynical than adult business executives. If you listen to our high-school seniors today, greed will be even more prevalent when they are running American industry.

On each of a dozen questions, seniors held to a lower standard of ethics—usually much lower—than did the adults whom they would one day succeed.

Building better mousetraps interests the seniors even less than it does those who run American industry today. The statement, "Prime objective of business is to produce the best product for the lowest price," won the agreement of one-third of the adult business people vs. only 27 percent of the high-school students.

★ **WHAT MIDDLE CLASS KIDS MISS: THE JOY OF GIVING**

"One of the most incredible things to me, really, is to see the typical middle class kid who's given everything he wants, except the privilege of service, the privilege of self-sacrifice, and the joy of being a giver. We've become a passive society that sees everything in terms of our open mouth—fill it with something! The idea that we can actually do things for something broader—a community—is lost."

★ —Willard Gaylin, bioethicist

Someone doing business with these high-school seniors is well-advised to get paid in advance:

"Do you think that a company which is going bankrupt has a moral obligation to repay its debt?" "Yes," said 56 percent of business executives. "No," said a larger majority (62 percent) of the seniors.

Similarly, almost all of the adults "would replace a faulty product made by [their] firm even if under no legal obligation to do so." Fewer of the seniors would do the right thing if they weren't under the gun of the law.

The kids on lying and cheating in business? They were twice as willing as the adults were to do one or the other in the course of business.

Would you "consider lying to achieve an important business objective of the firm?" "Yes," said two-thirds (66 percent) of the seniors vs. less than one-third (29 percent) of the adult executives.

"If a building is damaged by a storm, [would you] include all damages covered by insurance, even though not caused by storm?" "Yes," said half of the seniors vs. one-quarter (26 percent) of the grown-ups.

THE PRICE OF SUCCESS

"Success can be defined in so many ways. Right now people ask, how high is your position, how many people work for you, how high is your salary? When you get into that kind of yuppie version of success, you're going to sacrifice things along the way. There's not enough commitment to the ground rules of civic virtue. The yuppie is the constituency that makes it okay. They're the people who applaud success, who allow an Ivan Boesky to say, 'Greed is good,' and not be hooted down from the stage. They're the people who write books on how to win by intimidation and who can get on every TV show to teach people how to do that. Of course, this yuppie mentality is not really people, it's an approach. It's the philosophy of measuring our lives by what we get, what we acquire, who we know. It's a very shallow kind of life. People find that out in time. But during the period when that philosophy flourishes, we sacrifice a lot."

—Michael Josephson, ethicist

"Would you cheat on a highly important business certification test?" "Yes," said more than one-third (36 percent) of the seniors vs. 14 percent of the adults.

More than twice as many seniors said they thought that it was ethical to accept gifts—of $500 cash, or a vacation, or a Christmas present worth $100 or more—from a supplier with whom they were doing business.

More than twice as many (44 percent of the seniors vs. 21 percent of the adults) said that they would "make a deal if their brother-in-law has an inside tip that his company is being sold. There is no way you can get caught buying and selling the stock for a handsome profit."

Most of the seniors (59 percent) said that they would "consider making a deal that is borderline illegal but stand to make $10 million, and punishment is only six months' probation." Half as many adults (24 percent) agreed.

What are we to make of all this?

Taken at face value, it tells us that when these young people are running the show, they will probably spend their time gambling with other people's money while the American economy slides further down and we have to go to Germany or Japan to find a mousetrap that works.

Fortunately, there's some evidence that this is not the last word, even on how those same seniors will behave when they are in the real business world. They're not there yet, so what they say today is based not on experience but on messages they get from our current leaders and culture.

T E S T IV ★ ★ ★ ★ ★ ★ ★ ★ ★ ★

Many Americans use different interpretations of right and wrong at work and in their personal lives. How about you? Answer the yes-or-no questions below. Add up your score. Then see how you compare to the rest of America's work force.

ARE YOU AN HONEST WORKER?

1. You're certain that going to bed with one of your colleagues will advance your career. Would you do it?
2. Someone you work with asks you to cover while he or she takes a day off. Would you do it?
3. Do you think that exploring other job opportunities on company time is ethical?
4. Would you give your boss information that you know to be false?
5. Do you think that telling minor lies on a résumé is ethical?
6. You find out that a colleague is padding his or her expense account. Would you say anything?
7. Your boss gives you an order that involves your breaking the law. Would you obey the order?
8. Someone offers you a million dollars for your company's secrets. Would you accept the offer?
9. You find out that your boss is cheating your company. Would you say anything?
10. Have you ever taken the credit for someone else's work?
11. Would you lie to your boss to protect your job?
12. Would you ever conspire to get your boss's job?
13. You discover that your company is illegally dumping hazardous waste into the ocean. If you tell the authorities, you will risk the future of your company and all of its employees. Would you tell?
14. Have you ever taken home office supplies for your personal use?
15. Do you usually slack off a little when your boss isn't around?
16. Do you think that making personal calls on your company's phone is ethical?
17. Have you ever lied to your boss about one of your fellow workers?
18. Someone you know is using drugs at work. Would you say something?
19. Have you ever denigrated your boss to others?
20. You feel that your company is mistreating you. You know that you could sabotage its operations. Would you consider doing so to get even?

21. You find out that your best friend is stealing money from your company. Would you say something?
22. Do you always give 100 percent effort on the job?
23. If you were the boss, would you hire someone like you?

Give yourself one point for any of the following questions marked Yes: 6, 9, 13, 18, 21, 22, 23.

Give yourself one point for any of the following questions marked No: 1, 2, 3, 4, 5, 7, 8, 10, 11, 12, 14, 15, 16, 17, 19, 20.

Add up your score: _____.

NATIONAL RESULTS

	Percentage of the Population Who Scored		
Score	Above You	Below You	Rating
21–23	5%	95%	Ethical employee
20	10	90	
19	20	80	
18	30	70	
17	40	60	
16	50	50	
15	60	40	
14	70	30	
12–13	80	20	
10–11	90	10	
0–9	95	5	Unethical employee

VIII

COMMUNITY LIVES

23

Beverly Hills vs. the South Bronx: The Day They Told the Truth on Rodeo Drive

---

At two poles of American society lie Beverly Hills, in California, and the South Bronx, a distressed neighborhood in New York City.

Is it possible for one community to be "above" morality, while another is "below" it? We thought it would be fascinating to find out.

We were able to find out through the use of a test specially designed for these two communities. We did a series of confidential, in-depth interviews, then we tabulated the results: Beverly Hills vs. the South Bronx.

Beverly Hills is the coddled bedroom of the American dream factory. It's a place where you see limousines standing on quiet streets before the manicured lawns of mansions. Almost everyone is white. The average annual family income exceeds $100,000. Reported crimes against people in 1988 numbered 284, of which 3 were killings and 8 were rapes. The 14,805 residents have the services of 351 doctors, 121 dentists, and 536 legal firms.

The South Bronx is at the opposite end of the American spectrum. It is a place of littered streets lined by half-abandoned, gutted tenements. The people are mostly Hispanic and black. Few are white. The average annual family income is less than $10,000. The 2,014 reported crimes against people in 1988 included 25 murders and 47 rapes. At last count, there were 11 doctors, 13 dentists, and 2 law firms for 37,449 residents.

These are two extremes of the American experience.

We wanted to know in which area the residents are more prone to violence. Who uses illegal drugs more? Are the people of Beverly Hills morally superior to those in an American ghetto? But what we really wanted to find out was, how do the radical differences in their surroundings affect the sense of community of people in Beverly Hills and the South Bronx?

★   **WHAT HAPPENED WHEN WE CALLED THE POLICE FOR HELP**

When we called the Beverly Hills police for the official crime statistics, a very polite, friendly officer told us that he'd immediately tap into their computer system and fax us the information that day. He did. When we called the 41st Police Precinct in the South Bronx, a gruff police officer told us to "go bother the Police Commissioner."

★

Among the hundreds of people we interviewed in the South Bronx were a clerk, a cashier, a cook, a nurse's aide, a building superintendent, a dental hygiene therapist, a professional thief, an elementary-school teacher, a cab driver, and a philosopher.

Their counterparts in Beverly Hills included an oil company president, two film producers, an accountant, a physician, a pension fund administrator, and an engineer.

Here's what our modern *Tale Of Two Cities* revealed:

Legitimacy of the legal order.   People in the South Bronx absolutely reject the system of social and legal order. A high percentage, 49 percent, believe that "most of the laws in society are unfair . . . and we should not be forced to obey them." Only 14 percent of people in Beverly Hills agree with that point of view.

Official crime.   In 1988, there were ten times as many homicides, six times as many rapes, and five times as many robberies in the South Bronx as there were in Beverly Hills.

The police.   Forty-five percent of people in the South Bronx give the local police a failing grade. In Beverly Hills that percentage is only 33 percent.

Suicide.   Fifty-four percent of the people in Beverly Hills actually knew someone who committed suicide vs. 35 percent in the South Bronx.

And in Beverly Hills, a third more people than in the South Bronx have considered suicide themselves.

Child abuse. Sadly, child abuse is very common in the South Bronx. However, child abuse is just as common in Beverly Hills. The figures on child abuse are almost identical for both communities!

Infidelity. People in Beverly Hills are much more likely to have an extramarital affair (or two or three) than are people living in the South Bronx ghetto.

Drugs. The people in Beverly Hills are twice as likely to use illegal drugs as are the residents of the South Bronx. Thirty-eight percent of residents in Beverly Hills use illegal drugs vs. 17 percent in the Bronx.

Hidden crime. When we looked at unreported crimes, Beverly Hills residents were twice as likely to have actually committed a crime themselves. Beverly Hills residents were also more likely to personally know someone who has gone to jail.

Violence. Violence is certainly a fact of life in the South Bronx. But the average resident of Beverly Hills is four times as likely to own a gun. Twice as many reported that they had actually shot someone. Beverly Hills residents are as prone as residents of the South Bronx are to resorting to fistfights or shouting matches, but they are more likely (13 percent vs. 9 percent) to have sent someone to the hospital.

Charity. The 46 percent of people in the South Bronx who give to charity make a far greater sacrifice than do the 70 percent of wealthier residents of Beverly Hills, because they give much more on a percentage basis.

Not in my back yard. The principle of "not in my back yard" is considerably stronger in Beverly Hills than it is in the South Bronx. We asked residents in both places whether they would vote "Yes" or "No" to a proposal to locate certain kinds of institutions on the streets where they live. Whether it was a drug rehabilitation center, a shelter for the homeless, a home for the retarded, or an AIDS hospice, the not-on-my-street vote was greater, often twice as high, in Beverly Hills.

Capital crime and punishment. Capital crime is far more common in the South Bronx. However, the people of Beverly Hills are more vocal (70 percent vs. 52 percent) in support of the death penalty. A sizable number of people in Beverly Hills reported very harsh opinions on imposing legal death as well:

- Forty-three percent would execute an insane person
- Twenty-seven percent have no objection to executing the mentally retarded
- Twenty-three percent would execute a ten-year-old criminal

In the South Bronx, less than half as many people agreed.

The South Bronx has been depicted (several times by Hollywood) as a burnt-out shell of a community. In *Fort Apache the Bronx* and *The Bonfire of the Vanities*, the people were stereotyped as villains and *mal hombres*.

But we found the majority of people there to be honest and hardworking, trying to do their best under nearly impossible circumstances.

THE EXECUTIONERS

Among the women in Beverly Hills who would execute a ten-year-old criminal, we found a single college graduate in her early twenties, whose annual household income is more than $100,000. She gives nothing to charity but does give to panhandlers; would keep an envelope containing $100 that she found on the street; would not give half of a $20 million lottery hit to charity; and votes "No" on five of seven not-in-my-backyard questions. She rates her moral standing as "excellent" and her chances of heaven as "very good."

Among the Beverly Hills men who would execute a ten-year-old, is a single college graduate in his early twenties, whose household income is $75,000. He doesn't give to charity or to panhandlers. He voted "Not in my backyard" all the way.

Beverly Hills has its share of very good people too, but there is an unusually high degree of law-breaking and a high incidence of child abuse.

What of the future? Well, 54 percent of the adults in the South Bronx firmly believe that their children are growing up with stronger moral values than they have. In Beverly Hills, the number is 27 percent.

From our study, there is certainly no evidence that living in Beverly Hills results in being a better human being. On the contrary, on many counts, we had to score this one a moral victory for the people of the South Bronx.

24

The End of the Hometown in America: The End of Community

Somewhere in America's past, there is this wonderful, nearly perfect small town.

We've seen it pictured in the films of Frank Capra, in the paintings of Norman Rockwell. We've heard about it in *Oklahoma!* and even in Bruce Springsteen's songs.

In that town, everybody knows their neighbors. Tom Sawyer–style mischief is about as close as the town ever gets to real crime. In time of crisis, everyone pitches in, so no one in town is really alone.

That town was the American ideal community. It is also a faded dream now.

There are very few, if any, hometowns left anymore. More important, there is practically no sense of community to be found anywhere in this country.

A variety of facts support this sociological change in American living.

✶ | **WHITE PICKET FENCES**

"I love white picket fences. I think some of this country's greatest hours were the late 1940s and early 1950s, when there was some sort of fantastic mood that I've never seen again. Things seemed solid and clean and newer, and there was a depth of wholesomeness. . . . Life went to hell in a hand basket after that. Little kids were shooting heroin, not knowing where their mother was."

✶   —David Lynch, director of *Twin Peaks* and *Blue Velvet*

WHAT HAPPENED TO HOMETOWNS

As long as people respected the life and property of others, the social and public order somehow hung together.

Now Americans are losing respect for private property. Three in four of us confess to offenses against private property. We take things from work (60 percent). We steal a towel from a hotel or health club (50 percent). We don't repay loans (almost 25 percent). We shoplift (29 percent). We even steal from our spouses (9 percent), parents (21 percent), and friends (13 percent).

So here is what our current average neighborhood looks like. Here's what has probably occurred in your neighborhood in the past twelve months:

- Home burglary (48 percent of us have reported a "neighborhood" burglary recently)
- Car theft (35 percent)
- Drug dealing (27 percent)
- Murder or attempted murder (23 percent)
- Rape (9 percent)

Here's what your neighbors are afraid of:

- Being burglarized—we lock our doors (44 percent)
- Being raped (24 percent)
- Their cars being stolen (34 percent)
- Being murdered in the vicinity of their own homes (14 percent)

WE DON'T GET INVOLVED ANYMORE

Americans today have little or no sense of belonging to a community that is important to their lives. The thousands of people we interviewed averaged out their level of community involvement below three on a scale of one to ten.

And other measures of our alienation from community include:

- Two-thirds of us have never given any time at all to community activities or to the solving of community problems. Not surprisingly, more than two-thirds of us cannot name our local representative in Congress.
- More than half believe that they have no influence on the decisions made by local government.
- One-fourth admitted that they don't really give a damn about any of their neighborhood's problems.

CHARITY BEGINS AT HOME

We are not a charitable people right now. The average American gives considerably less than 1 percent of his or her income to charity. Nearly one-third of all Americans have never given money to *any* charitable cause!

★ **BY REGION: WHERE CHARITABLE DONATIONS ARE MADE**

(For a map of America's regions, see Part I.)

★ GIVEN MONEY TO A CHARITABLE ORGANIZATION (National Average: 69%)

Region	Percentage Who Donate to Charity	Region	Percentage Who Donate to Charity
New South	75%	Rust Belt	69%
New England	75	Marlboro Country	62
Granary	71	L.A.–Mex	62
Metropolis	70	Pac Rim	57
Old Dixie	69		

★

As you travel the country, though, there is a significant difference, region to region, in our willingness to give. Charitable fund-raisers' prospects are best in the New South and New England, poorest in the Pac Rim and L.A.–Mex.

WHO ARE THE PEOPLE NEXT DOOR?

We don't know our neighbors, either. The great majority of Americans (72 percent) openly admit that they don't know the people next door:

- Have never spent an evening with them (45 percent)
- Have never borrowed the proverbial cup of sugar, or anything else (42 percent)
- Have never been inside their homes (27 percent)
- Don't even know the names of the people who live next door (15 percent)

✶ | **WHO'LL CARE FOR THE ELDERLY?**

Inside our communities, how about the elderly? We asked our respondents, "Whose responsibility is it to care for the elderly?" Their heartfelt responses:

Whose Responsibility	Percentage
The children	54%
Government	21
The elderly themselves	20
Charitable organizations	3

We asked people if they thought that their children would take care of them in their old age. Forty-six percent of those asked said "No."

25

America's Real Crime Statistics

America's official statistics on crime are somewhat misleading. According to our research crime is underestimated by about 600 percent.

Thirty-nine percent of the people in America have some kind of criminal offense in their past, and a sizable number seem to actually draw the lightning of violence on themselves.

Crimes of violence were confessed by enough of our respondents to persuade us that the proportion of our population prone to violence is much higher than any national statistics released to this point.

In this land of violence, it came as no great surprise that only a minority of us (32 percent) feel very safe in our neighborhoods. The rest confess that "we live with continual fear."

Our fears are grounded in the facts of our daily lives, the real crime statistics that come from our own experience.

More than half of all Americans (60 percent) have been the victims of crime at least once in their lives. *Of those, more than half (58 percent) have been victimized twice or more.*

The statistics of violence in our poorer neighborhoods are familiar fare

★ | **OFFICIAL STATISTICS UNDERESTIMATE CRIME BY 600 PERCENT**

COMPARISON OF OUR CRIME STATISTICS WITH OFFICIAL CRIME STATISTICS

★ The dimensions of the crime problem in America are very big indeed. According to the U.S. Bureau of Crime Statistics, there were 20 million personal crimes (that is, crimes against individual Americans) in 1988 alone. This means that in 1988, there were 100 personal crimes for every 1,000 Americans!

As bad as these figures may seem, they underestimate the real crime threat to most Americans. Crime statistics are calculated on a yearly basis, meaning that the official statistics only report the chances that an individual American was victimized in one given year.

★ We decided to take a different approach, asking Americans if they had ever been the victims of a crime. We were sure that the number would be much higher than the official single-year averages, but we were unprepared for the revelation that fully 60 percent or 600 in every 1,000 adult Americans have been the victim of at least one crime.

This figure is six times greater than the single-year official estimates. We further found that 350 in every 1,000 Americans have been the victims of at least two crimes (3.5 times the single-year estimate) and that 200 Americans in every 1,000 have been the victims of at least three crimes.

For the record, the 100-in-1,000 official crime-victimization rate corresponds almost exactly to our estimate of the number of Americans who have been the victims of four or more crimes in their lives.

in our newspapers. What surprised us is the experience of crime reported by people who live in America's upper-middle-class and rich neighborhoods:

In our Beverly Hills–South Bronx study, for example, we found that the people of Beverly Hills are almost as likely (53 percent vs. 55 percent) to have been victims of crime as the people of the South Bronx; the people of Beverly Hills are almost as likely (12 percent vs. 14 percent) to have experienced a crime of violence themselves. People in Beverly Hills are also more likely (50 percent vs. 48 percent) to know someone who has been struck by violence.

TRUE CONFESSIONS OF CRIME

All kinds of people confessed small-scale crimes in the privacy of our interviews:

- A bank teller from Metropolis: "Lots of petty theft when I was a teenager. Now I work in a bank, right."

ericans go beyond simple advocacy in their support of the
y.

n in four wants a return to public executions, although this
nodern manner—on television.

of the people we spoke to would like to witness an execution

ercent would pull the switch themselves. These volunteer
are men and women from the whole spectrum of American

g of the men includes a flower-shop owner in his early
ree-times-married school teacher; a postal supervisor in his
a nuclear plant supervisor; an insurance executive; several
tors; a young, professional model; and lawyers from San
'ashington, and Mississippi.

e women would-be executioners are two legal secretaries;
of a pizza parlor; doctors, lawyers, and psychologists.

- A Rust Belt lawyer: "Drugs and theft right up to the present time. I sometimes steal at our office."
- A Southern cop: "I've stolen many items. Little here, little there."
- A receptionist from a rural area in the Northeast: "When I was younger, I stole from department stores. I occasionally hit the malls now."
- A high-school coach from the East: "I stole a leather jacket last year. Every couple of years, I steal something big."
- A young woman from New England, who is a fitness instructor: "Attempted larceny. Also, stealing gasoline from cars in the neighborhood."
- A meat cutter from the Midwest: "Dope-stealing from work."
- A Midwestern woman, who owns a manicuring business: "Stealing in stores and buying drugs."
- A Midwestern woman, who now is president of a small company: "Stole paper goods, pens, small machines from a former employer."
- A broker for the federal government: "As a teen, working in a camera shop, I stole a lot of equipment."
- An Old Dixie factory foreman: "I steal packs of cigarettes off our lunch wagon."
- A realtor from the West Coast: "Smoked marijuana and committed petty theft in convenience stores."
- A mother of two from the Rust Belt: "Stole cosmetics at a Mary Kay show."

★ **MAMA TRIED**

" 'This is the nineties, man. We're the type of people who don't take no for an answer. If your mom says no to a kid in the nineties, the kid's just going to laugh'—a twenty-one-year-old surfer called Road Dog, who said his family owned a chain of pharmacies.

★ "He and his friends shouted in appreciation as another gang member lifted his long hair to reveal a tattoo on a bare shoulder: 'Mama Tried.' "
—*New York Times*, April 10, 1990

Others confessing to regular stealing: a college president, a telephone interviewer, a licensed practical nurse, an auto mechanic, an insurance salesman, a market-research interviewer, a waitress, the owner of an insurance agency, a postal supervisor, a filmmaker, a mailman, a carpet installer, a market consultant, a home health aide.

More serious crime is committed by a disturbingly large number of people we talked to.

Fully 2 percent of our nationally projectable sample admit to having pushed drugs; another 1 percent each to robbery, car theft, and assault. That's a lot of people across this country who have been involved in felonies.

THE PERENNIAL VICTIM

One American in ten has suffered four or more crimes in his or her lifetime. We decided to take a closer look at perennial victims. Why do some people seem to walk under a raincloud?

They are not people whose circumstances make them more vulnerable than most. Something else is going on, something that has to do with who they are as human beings.

That's the conclusion we were led to when we discovered who the perennial victims are *not*:

- They are *not* more than averagely poor or uneducated or members of minorities.
- They are *not* mostly women (60 percent are men).
- They are *not* mostly old (only 6 percent are sixty years old or older).

In fact, the greatest proportion of perennial victims shows up in the age group where you might least expect to find them: men between thirty-five and forty-four.

None of that fits with the standard perception about where crime hits hardest in America.

Who are these perennial crime victims then?

- They're more than twice as likely to have committed a crime themselves. Fifty-nine percent admit to having committed at least one crime.
- They're more than twice as likely (51 percent vs. 20 percent) to have contemplated suicide. Almost half have been in therapy.

Most interestingly, perennial crime victims are often victims of child abuse. They are three times as likely to have been beaten and four times as likely to have been sexually abused as children.

WHAT AMERICA REALLY BELIEV

Americans kill each other at a fa 25,000 homicides reported each ye industrial country. Maybe it is na penalty, abolished throughout Weste the United States.

The number of prisoners on de support for the death penalty is in right now about the death penalty:

We found that two-thirds of our execution.

A number of Americans go be vengeance, or some kind of justice.

When it comes to specific offens penalty comes close to 100 percent.

Crimes against children—even w those for which the largest number

---

✶ | **SELLING TRADE SECRETS TO JAPAN?**
AMERICANS NOW SAY, "HANG 'EM H

Nearly as many (41 percent) American a form of treason as worthy of execu (49 percent).

✶ | **AMERICANS SUPPORT THE DEATH PE**

Offense

Ran a child-prostitution ring
Sold drugs to children
Killed an innocent child
✶ Engaged in senseless mass-murder
Killed a policeman
Was a terrorist who planted a bomb o
Put poison in over-the-counter drugs
Killed a storekeeper in a robbery
Killed someone while driving drunk
✶ Raped a woman
Sold military secrets to the Soviets
Sold trade secrets to the Japanese

Many Ar
death penal
One pers
time in the
One-third
themselves.
Fully 34
executioner
life.
A sampli
thirties; a t
early forties
medical de
Francisco, V
Among t
the manage

26

Poverty: The Forgotten Crusade

Once upon a time, there was a war on poverty. That was in the 1960s.

In those days, many idealistic people thought that such a war could be won—that most poverty could eventually be ended in America. What ended, of course, was not poverty but the war against it. It came to an abrupt close with the end of the presidency of Lyndon B. Johnson.

Like the war in Vietnam, the war on poverty ended without victory and without agreement on the reasons for its failure. As was the case in Vietnam, some thought that the war on poverty failed because we did not give the task the resources needed for victory.

A quarter-century later, the poor are with us in growing numbers. In the opinion of most of us, they always will be. Ninety-two percent among us believe that poverty will not be eliminated.

The pessimism runs very deep and right to a core problem. Three-fourths of us believe that the government doesn't know how to win such a struggle, even if we were willing to spend whatever it takes.

Once again, we see ourselves having potential and resources but not the leadership to get essential jobs done.

There was a time when people in foreign countries thought of America as the land where the streets were paved with gold. Now our city streets are those of "the New Calcutta," which is what one New York newspaper frequently calls its hometown.

A Japanese businessman who visited our country had this to report: "Poverty is very visible all over America, everywhere I travel, especially among blacks and Hispanics. It is appalling for me to see, but Americans seem immune to it."

Our emotions about the poor are hopelessly mixed up. Many of us are sympathetic. The great majority (84 percent) say that the poor do not deserve their poverty. Close to two-thirds think that the poor are treated unfairly; a larger majority find it unfair that the wealthy get better health care. Almost three-fourths say that they are more sympathetic to the poor than they were five years ago.

★ WHAT THE AMERICAN GOVERNMENT OWES THE POOR

Middle-class-and-above Americans (the Haves) feel very differently than do the Have-Nots about what the poor deserve in this country.

Item	Percentage Who Believe That the Government Should Help	
	The Have-Nots	The Haves
Enough food	81%	72%
A place to live	80	63
Heat and water	75	65
A job	67	43
Money	58	24
Day care	47	40
Air-conditioning	32	7

However, in our actions, we often turn a harsh face to poor people. The majority of Americans believe that the poor are simply not willing to make the personal sacrifices required to get ahead, for example, that people on welfare could find work if they really wanted to. Many of us (42 percent) believe that the poor are poor because they are lazy, or due to faults of their own—opinions that seem inconsistent with the stated belief that the poor don't deserve their poverty.

Many people confessed that they have a real contempt for the poor. The poor themselves feel that contempt more than most of us do, and twice as much as the rich do.

- A Rust Belt lawyer: "Drugs and theft right up to the present time. I sometimes steal at our office."
- A Southern cop: "I've stolen many items. Little here, little there."
- A receptionist from a rural area in the Northeast: "When I was younger, I stole from department stores. I occasionally hit the malls now."
- A high-school coach from the East: "I stole a leather jacket last year. Every couple of years, I steal something big."
- A young woman from New England, who is a fitness instructor: "Attempted larceny. Also, stealing gasoline from cars in the neighborhood."
- A meat cutter from the Midwest: "Dope-stealing from work."
- A Midwestern woman, who owns a manicuring business: "Stealing in stores and buying drugs."
- A Midwestern woman, who now is president of a small company: "Stole paper goods, pens, small machines from a former employer."
- A broker for the federal government: "As a teen, working in a camera shop, I stole a lot of equipment."
- An Old Dixie factory foreman: "I steal packs of cigarettes off our lunch wagon."
- A realtor from the West Coast: "Smoked marijuana and committed petty theft in convenience stores."
- A mother of two from the Rust Belt: "Stole cosmetics at a Mary Kay show."

★ | **MAMA TRIED**

" 'This is the nineties, man. We're the type of people who don't take no for an answer. If your mom says no to a kid in the nineties, the kid's just going to laugh'—a twenty-one-year-old surfer called Road Dog, who said his family owned a chain of pharmacies.

★ | "He and his friends shouted in appreciation as another gang member lifted his long hair to reveal a tattoo on a bare shoulder: 'Mama Tried.' "
—*New York Times,* April 10, 1990

Others confessing to regular stealing: a college president, a telephone interviewer, a licensed practical nurse, an auto mechanic, an insurance salesman, a market-research interviewer, a waitress, the owner of an insurance agency, a postal supervisor, a filmmaker, a mailman, a carpet installer, a market consultant, a home health aide.

More serious crime is committed by a disturbingly large number of people we talked to.

Fully 2 percent of our nationally projectable sample admit to having pushed drugs; another 1 percent each to robbery, car theft, and assault. That's a lot of people across this country who have been involved in felonies.

THE PERENNIAL VICTIM

One American in ten has suffered four or more crimes in his or her lifetime. We decided to take a closer look at perennial victims. Why do some people seem to walk under a raincloud?

They are not people whose circumstances make them more vulnerable than most. Something else is going on, something that has to do with who they are as human beings.

That's the conclusion we were led to when we discovered who the perennial victims are *not*:

- They are *not* more than averagely poor or uneducated or members of minorities.
- They are *not* mostly women (60 percent are men).
- They are *not* mostly old (only 6 percent are sixty years old or older).

In fact, the greatest proportion of perennial victims shows up in the age group where you might least expect to find them: men between thirty-five and forty-four.

None of that fits with the standard perception about where crime hits hardest in America.

Who are these perennial crime victims then?

- They're more than twice as likely to have committed a crime themselves. Fifty-nine percent admit to having committed at least one crime.
- They're more than twice as likely (51 percent vs. 20 percent) to have contemplated suicide. Almost half have been in therapy.

Most interestingly, perennial crime victims are often victims of child abuse. They are three times as likely to have been beaten and four times as likely to have been sexually abused as children.

WHAT AMERICA REALLY BELIEVES ABOUT THE DEATH PENALTY

Americans kill each other at a far higher rate (currently, more than 25,000 homicides reported each year) than do the citizens of any other industrial country. Maybe it is natural that sentiment for the death penalty, abolished throughout Western Europe, is making a comeback in the United States.

The number of prisoners on death row rises each year, and public support for the death penalty is increasing. Here's what people believe right now about the death penalty:

We found that two-thirds of our respondents (68 percent) favor legal execution.

A number of Americans go beyond that in their desire for legal vengeance, or some kind of justice.

When it comes to specific offenses, Americans' support for the death penalty comes close to 100 percent.

Crimes against children—even when they do not involve murder—are those for which the largest number advocate death.

✶ | **SELLING TRADE SECRETS TO JAPAN?**
AMERICANS NOW SAY, "HANG 'EM HIGH."

Nearly as many (41 percent) Americans now consider selling trade secrets to Japan a form of treason as worthy of execution as selling military secrets to the Soviets (49 percent).

✶ | **AMERICANS SUPPORT THE DEATH PENALTY OVERWHELMINGLY**

Offense	Percentage Supporting Execution
Ran a child-prostitution ring	97%
Sold drugs to children	95
Killed an innocent child	83
Engaged in senseless mass-murder	82
Killed a policeman	78
Was a terrorist who planted a bomb on an airplane	75
Put poison in over-the-counter drugs	74
Killed a storekeeper in a robbery	73
Killed someone while driving drunk	70
Raped a woman	59
Sold military secrets to the Soviets	49
Sold trade secrets to the Japanese	41

Many Americans go beyond simple advocacy in their support of the death penalty.

One person in four wants a return to public executions, although this time in the modern manner—on television.

One-third of the people we spoke to would like to witness an execution themselves.

Fully 34 percent would pull the switch themselves. These volunteer executioners are men and women from the whole spectrum of American life.

A sampling of the men includes a flower-shop owner in his early thirties; a three-times-married school teacher; a postal supervisor in his early forties; a nuclear plant supervisor; an insurance executive; several medical doctors; a young, professional model; and lawyers from San Francisco, Washington, and Mississippi.

Among the women would-be executioners are two legal secretaries; the manager of a pizza parlor; doctors, lawyers, and psychologists.

26

Poverty: The Forgotten
Crusade

Once upon a time, there was a war on poverty. That was in the 1960s.

In those days, many idealistic people thought that such a war could be won—that most poverty could eventually be ended in America. What ended, of course, was not poverty but the war against it. It came to an abrupt close with the end of the presidency of Lyndon B. Johnson.

Like the war in Vietnam, the war on poverty ended without victory and without agreement on the reasons for its failure. As was the case in Vietnam, some thought that the war on poverty failed because we did not give the task the resources needed for victory.

A quarter-century later, the poor are with us in growing numbers. In the opinion of most of us, they always will be. Ninety-two percent among us believe that poverty will not be eliminated.

The pessimism runs very deep and right to a core problem. Three-fourths of us believe that the government doesn't know how to win such a struggle, even if we were willing to spend whatever it takes.

Once again, we see ourselves having potential and resources but not the leadership to get essential jobs done.

179

There was a time when people in foreign countries thought of America as the land where the streets were paved with gold. Now our city streets are those of "the New Calcutta," which is what one New York newspaper frequently calls its hometown.

A Japanese businessman who visited our country had this to report: "Poverty is very visible all over America, everywhere I travel, especially among blacks and Hispanics. It is appalling for me to see, but Americans seem immune to it."

Our emotions about the poor are hopelessly mixed up. Many of us are sympathetic. The great majority (84 percent) say that the poor do not deserve their poverty. Close to two-thirds think that the poor are treated unfairly; a larger majority find it unfair that the wealthy get better health care. Almost three-fourths say that they are more sympathetic to the poor than they were five years ago.

★ WHAT THE AMERICAN GOVERNMENT OWES THE POOR

Middle-class-and-above Americans (the Haves) feel very differently than do the Have-Nots about what the poor deserve in this country.

Item	Percentage Who Believe That the Government Should Help	
	The Have-Nots	The Haves
Enough food	81%	72%
A place to live	80	63
Heat and water	75	65
A job	67	43
Money	58	24
Day care	47	40
Air-conditioning	32	7

However, in our actions, we often turn a harsh face to poor people. The majority of Americans believe that the poor are simply not willing to make the personal sacrifices required to get ahead, for example, that people on welfare could find work if they really wanted to. Many of us (42 percent) believe that the poor are poor because they are lazy, or due to faults of their own—opinions that seem inconsistent with the stated belief that the poor don't deserve their poverty.

Many people confessed that they have a real contempt for the poor. The poor themselves feel that contempt more than most of us do, and twice as much as the rich do.

Am I my brother's keeper? Are the poor actually members of my community? Americans are evenly divided on this crucial social question. Just over half feel a moral obligation to help the poor; just under half do not feel any obligation to help.

The people of New England and Metropolis, known for their liberalism, actually feel the least obligation to help the poor. The spirit of charity and social obligation is greatest in Marlboro Country, theoretically the true home of the rugged individualist, and in the L.A.–Mex and Old Dixie regions.

OUR BOTTOM LINE ON THE POOR

Few among us feel a personal obligation or that the buck stops with us. Asked who is responsible for helping the poor, half pointed to the poor themselves; a quarter said it was the government; and for 8 percent, it was the community.

"I, myself" got the vote of just 7 percent of the Americans we talked to.

★ BY REGION: WHO BELIEVES IN HELPING THE POOR

(For a map of America's regions, see Part I.)

WE HAVE A MORAL RESPONSIBILITY TO HELP THE POOR (National Average: 55%)

Region	Percentage Who Agree	Region	Percentage Who Agree
Marlboro Country	69%	Rust Belt	54%
L.A.–Mex	68	Pac Rim	51
Old Dixie	67	Metropolis	46
New South	56	New England	33
Granary	54		

27

The New Racism:
White and Black

In the hit movie *Do The Right Thing*, Mookie (played by the black director Spike Lee) curses out one of his Italian bosses at the Brooklyn pizzeria where they work: "Dago, wop, garlic-breath, pizza-slinging, spaghetti-bending, Vic Damone, Perry Como, Luciano Pavarotti, *Sole Mio*-nonsinging motherfucker," Mookie says.

To which his young Italian boss retorts, "You gold-teeth, gold-chain-wearing, fried-chicken-and-biscuit-eatin', monkey, ape, baboon, big-thigh, fast-running, high-jumping, spear-chucking, spade moulanyan, you."

Spike Lee's symbolic confrontation still happens today, but not as much as it used to. In a way, it's an anachronistic scene, but it speaks to the new reality: a subtler and much more hypocritical racism.

THERE IS A NEW RACISM IN AMERICA

In some ways, the dream of brotherhood seems even more distant now than when Martin Luther King, Jr., spoke from the steps of the Lincoln Memorial in 1963.

"I have a dream," King said in one of the best-remembered American speeches of our time. "I have a dream that one day, on the red hills of Georgia, the sons of former slaves and the sons of former slave owners will be able to sit together at the table of brotherhood."

It seems so very long ago, because in the 1990s, white Americans hold blacks, and blacks alone, to blame for their current position in American society. "We tried to help," whites say over and over, "but blacks wouldn't help themselves." This is the basis for what we've called the new racism. Everything flows from it. It is a change from the hardcore racism that existed in our country's earlier years. It is also a dramatic contrast to the attitudes of the 1960s, when many whites, from the President on down, publicly stated that black people were owed compensation for centuries of oppression.

★ **1990s STEREOTYPES: WHITES ON BLACKS vs. BLACKS ON WHITES**

ATTRIBUTES WHITES ASSOCIATE WITH BLACKS:

Attribute	Percentage Who Agree	Attribute	Percentage Who Agree
Athletic	61%	Dangerous	30%
Criminal	33	Lazy	29
Poor	32	Vulgar	22
Violent	31	Dirty	14

ATTRIBUTES BLACKS ASSOCIATE WITH WHITES:

Attribute	Percentage Who Agree	Attribute	Percentage Who Agree
Racist	49%	Intelligent	14%
Wealthy	29	Dangerous	14
Greedy	21		

In our interviews, a majority of whites told us what they really think: that white America has taken enough blame for the low economic status of blacks and that from now on, it's up to the blacks themselves to improve their lot.

Two-thirds of us now believe that a black person has the same chance of success as a white. "If blacks are poor, it's because they haven't taken advantage of the opportunities America offers them."

It's that black-and-white an issue for most whites.

To three-fourths of white people, the recent success of Asian-Americans absolutely confirms their low opinion of blacks.

"If blacks would only work as hard as Asians, they would succeed": that's the lesson that most whites draw from the Asian experience. But then, as 68 percent also told us, some races are harder-working than others.

For most Americans, racial brotherhood is not a dream—it's a nightmare. From the stereotypes that blacks and whites see when they look at each other, it's not surprising that whites and blacks don't want to be "brothers."

Most whites (54 percent) privately admit that they hold one or more of these racist opinions:

- Blacks are more violent than whites (44 percent).
- Whites are clearly more intelligent than blacks (22 percent).
- The Ku Klux Klan has legitimate grievances (20 percent).
- Whites have a right to keep blacks out of their neighborhoods entirely (15 percent).
- Whites would refuse a blood transfusion from a black (19 percent).
- Whites would demand a white doctor if a hospital assigned a black to them (13 percent).

Most whites move in racist circles. More than half openly admit that they have racist friends. They also say that their neighbors would be extremely upset if they sold their home to a black family.

White reluctance to associate with blacks rises dramatically when sex is involved:

- Whites could never get romantically involved with a black person (77 percent).
- Whites would object if their son or daughter brought home a black date (50 percent).
- Whites become angry when they see a black man walking hand-in-hand with a white woman (41 percent).

Racist attitudes among whites still vary tremendously around the country. You're more than fifteen times as likely to find a hardcore racist, someone with strongly antiblack attitudes, among residents of Old Dixie as on the Pac Rim. With the exception of New England, white people are much more racist east of the Mississippi than they are west of it.

But the good news is that there are fewer hardcore racists than ever before.

★ | **BY REGION: WHERE THE HARDCORE RACISTS LIVE**

(For a map of America's regions, see Part I.)

WHO THE HARDCORE RACISTS ARE (National Average: 10%)

Region	Percentage of Hardcore Racists	Region	Percentage of Hardcore Racists
Old Dixie	15%	Granary	6%
Rust Belt	14	L.A.–Mex	4
Metropolis	13	New England	3
New South	12	Pac Rim	1
Marlboro Country	8		

★ | **AUTHORITY FIGURES FOR WHITES AND BLACKS**

Whom Americans believe when told what is right and wrong:

Who Is Believed	Percentage Who Believe	
	Whites	Blacks
Spouse/lover	53%	66%
Parent	44	61
Grandparent	35	60
Best friend	35	53
Child	30	47
Minister/priest/rabbi	29	49
Government	23	37
Boss	21	36
Teacher	21	42
The President	17	33
Neighbor	7	17
Famous athlete	7	15
TV minister	5	23
TV personality	5	12

In the old Confederacy, the face of white racism is definitely changing. Traditionalist Old Dixie still ranks first in hardcore racism, and yet in some respects, white attitudes are uglier in the industrializing New South. New South whites scored higher than did whites in Old Dixie on every negative quality they associate with blacks.

How about you? Test V at the end of this chapter reveals how your true attitudes on race compare with those of others across the country.

★ | **CHURCH AS A MORAL GUIDE FOR WHITES AND BLACKS**

Percent looking to church for religious guidance:

| | Percentage | |
Issue	Whites	Blacks
Homelessness	53%	73%
Racism in America	49	68
Fighting poverty	49	64
The drug problem	48	72
Civil rights	42	61
ERA	32	50
Affirmative action	30	53
Protecting the rights of criminals	30	51
Book banning	30	41
School busing	26	46

THE REAL-LIFE MORALS OF BLACK PEOPLE

Black people show themselves to be less influenced by the enormous changes now taking place in American morals. More blacks have kept what so many whites have lost: a belief in moral authorities.

Blacks are far more religious than whites. When we asked which guidelines people would choose in a conflict among the Constitution, religious beliefs, and personal ethics, more than twice as many blacks said that they would follow their religion. Half as many blacks would follow their own sense of right and wrong.

On issues of the day, black people, much more than whites, look to their churches for guidance. This applies to a wide range of issues both spiritual and temporal. On not one issue (not even on racism in America) are blacks less likely than whites to follow their churches.

It's not just religion. Black people are much more willing to accept the judgment of others on questions of right and wrong. Whether from a spouse or lover, or from a TV personality, blacks showed themselves more willing, usually by a wide margin, to follow another person's moral lead.

The much-discussed disintegration of the black family finds confirmation in what people told us.

More than whites, blacks believe that marriage will be obsolete by the year 2000, that most spouses cheat, and that most marriages end in divorce.

They are twice as likely as whites to think that their spouses are cheating, to admit that they themselves are cheating, and to predict that their own marriages will end in divorce.

Fewer blacks than whites (35 percent vs. 42 percent) have ever actually used drugs.

When it comes to serious alcohol problems, however, there is close to racial equality: whites at 24 percent vs. blacks at 21 percent.

Blacks are even more pessimistic than whites about heroes in America. Only two blacks in ten can name a single leader they admire.

And yet, have we made progress in the area of race? Blacks admit that there is more opportunity for them now. There definitely aren't as many hardcore racists as there used to be in this country. So the answer is probably "Yes." We have come a half-step forward on the issue of race. There has been slow progress. The dream of Martin Luther King is still alive.

T E S T V ★ ★ ★ ★ ★ ★ ★ ★ ★ ★

Among the white people who make up the majority in America, attitudes toward black people range from the extreme prejudice of the Ku Klux Klan to the self-sacrifice of the civil rights workers of the 1960s. If you're white, where do you rate yourself? And where are you really? To find out, take the test below. Answer the yes-or-no questions. Then add up your score and find out how you compare. Are you less racist than most white people or more so? Does what you believe about yourself hold up to the test of reality?

ARE YOU A RACIST?

1. Do you believe that this country would have fewer racial problems if whites and blacks would each keep to their own kind?
2. You learn after an accident that you have received a blood transfusion from a black person. Would that bother you?
3. Have you ever had a black person in your home for a social occasion?
4. How do you think your friends would react if you married a black person? Would they be understanding?
5. Do you have any black friends?
6. The political party that you normally support nominates for President a black candidate who, in your opinion, is otherwise fully qualified. Would you vote for this candidate?
7. Many Asian-Americans have succeeded in this country. Would you conclude that blacks could be equally successful if they worked equally hard?
8. Do you believe that you could fall in love with a black person?
9. Do you go to restaurants or bars in which blacks are made to feel uncomfortable?
10. Do you believe that the United States has an obligation to compensate blacks for discrimination suffered in the past through affirmative action, even if such programs sometimes put white Americans at a disadvantage?
11. Do you believe that blacks are naturally superior to whites as athletes?
12. Would you be reluctant to adopt a black child?
13. Suppose you sold your home to a black family. Do you think that your neighbors would be upset?
14. Do you think that a black person has as good a chance as a white person does to succeed in today's America?
15. Do you think that blacks are more likely than whites to resort to violence?

16. Is there a black person who you believe is qualified to be President of the United States?
17. Do you think that white people should have the right to keep blacks out of white neighborhoods?
18. Do you think that whites are more intelligent than blacks?
19. Do you think that people of some races are harder-working than others?
20. Do you think that people who advocate white supremacy are un-American?
21. Do you think that black people feel uncomfortable around you?
22. Do you consider any of your friends to be racists?
23. Do you believe that blacks are poor because they fail to take advantage of the opportunities open to them?
24. Do you believe that some of the Ku Klux Klan's grievances are legitimate?
25. The hospital assigns you a black doctor. Would you request that he be replaced by a white doctor?
26. Do you approve of the court decisions that have forced black children to attend white schools?
27. Would you object to working for a boss who is black?
28. Would you send your children to a private school that doesn't admit blacks?
29. "White Americans have taken enough blame for the plight of blacks. It's time blacks took responsibility for their own fate." Do you agree?
30. Do you feel uncomfortable around black people?
31. Do you believe that we as a nation should spend less time on the problems of blacks and more on the problems faced by all Americans?
32. Do you think that it was a mistake to honor Martin Luther King, Jr., with a national holiday?
33. Does it make you uneasy to see a black man walking hand-in-hand with a white woman?
34. Your son or daughter brings home a black date for dinner. Would you object?
35. You are walking down the street late at night. You see a black teenaged boy on your side of the street, a white on the other side. Would you cross the street?
36. Do you think that Mikhail Gorbachev is more qualified than Jesse Jackson to be President of the United States?

Give yourself one point for any of the following questions marked Yes: 1, 2, 7, 9, 11, 12, 13, 14, 15, 17, 18, 19, 21, 22, 23, 24, 25, 27, 28, 29, 30, 31, 32, 33, 34, 35, 36.

Give yourself one point for any of the following questions marked No: 3, 4, 5, 6, 8, 10, 16, 20, 26.

Add up your score: _____ .

NATIONAL RESULTS

	Percentage of the Population Who Scored		
Score	Above You	Below You	Rating
22–36	5%	95%	Hardcore racist
20–21	10	90	
18–19	20	80	
16–17	30	70	
15	40	60	
13–14	50	50	
12	60	40	
11	70	30	
8– 9	80	20	
5– 7	90	10	
0– 4	95	5	Color-blind

28

★ ★ ★ ★ ★

America's Most Dangerous Addictions

THE NUMBER ONE DRUG

Alcohol is America's most serious drug by far. It has been that way for years. Close to 30 million Americans report having had a drinking problem.

Over 19 million Americans admit that they have had serious alcohol problems in the past. Another 11 million of us are having alcohol problems right now. Alcohol abusers make trouble for others too: One-third of all adults have personally suffered from someone else's drinking.

More than two-thirds of the people we spoke to told us that alcohol hurt them in one or more of the following ways:

They've lost good friends or lovers; wasted money they couldn't afford to; suffered liver and kidney and other health problems; did things they would later regret; got into trouble with the law; lost a job; got into an accident; suffered depression, anger, embarrassment.

More than half of all respondents told us that they'd driven while drunk—but only one in four got caught at it.

Men are more prone than women are to drinking problems; gays and

---

★ | **WHERE BOOZE AND RUBBER MEET THE ROAD**

★

- About 25,000 Americans are killed each year by drunk drivers.
- Drunk drivers are the number-one killer of Americans under the age of forty.
- About 450,000 youths are arrested year after year for driving under the influence of alcohol.
- About 56 percent of Americans have reported driving while intoxicated.
- Only 14 percent of drunk drivers have ever been caught.

---

bisexuals more than straights; Catholics and Protestants much more than Jews.

Alcohol abuse is more common among those who haven't graduated from college; liberals more than conservatives; the divorced and single more than the married; the poor more than the rich.

Thoughts for driving home late on a Saturday night: You are likeliest to meet a drunk driver in the Granary section of the country. That is followed by Marlboro Country and the Pac Rim. You're safest in New England and, believe it or not, in Metropolis. So, in spite of all the publicity, warnings, and severe penalties, there are still plenty of "DWIs" (driving while intoxicated) on the road. They are following their own moral codes. They believe that drinking and driving is all right for them.

America lives in a state of denial about its drinking problem. The

---

★ | **AMERICA'S TOP 10 DRUGS OF CHOICE**
(Not Including Alcohol)

Drug	Percentage of Drug Users	
	People Who Have Ever Been Users	People Who Are Current Users
Marijuana	35%	23%
Cocaine	15	6
LSD/acid	10	1
Speed/diet pills	7	*
Downers	3	*
Hashish	3	*
Crack	2	*
Heroin	1	*
Crystal methamphetamine (speed)	*	*
Ecstasy	*	*

*Less than 1 percent

majority of us feel that we can handle alcohol, even those who admit to having serious drinking problems. All of which suggests that we really have a drinking problem.

THE "DRUG WARS"

We've all heard a lot about the war on drugs. It has become one of our national priorities. And as people see it, it's drugs other than alcohol which are leading us into moral decline. Eight-five percent of Americans believe that the drug problem is more serious now than in the past. Right now, Americans believe that seven in ten crimes are caused by drugs.

That simply isn't so.

America actually has two different drug cultures.

America's Recreational Drug Users:
41 Percent of Us

Recreational drug use, rooted in the counterculture of the 1960s, usually involves marijuana and some cocaine. It affects a lot of people—41 percent of our respondents admit that they've tried either marijuana or cocaine.

The Crack Culture

The other drug culture is the one we see depicted on the TV news. It is the crack and heroin culture of our inner-city ghettoes. At this time, it's limited to a relatively small number of people, but it destroys lives and ravages communities. It has made our nation's capital a national disgrace and even drove that city's mayor from office.

Still, crack and heroin are relatively minor drugs in terms of numbers of users. Marijuana and cocaine are by far the drugs most frequently used today.

And drug use varies considerably around the country. There are more druggies in the Pac Rim and New England than elsewhere. Marijuana is the drug of choice. Pot is a noncriminal offense in Oregon, and New England is full of universities where it is habitual.

Old Dixie and Marlboro Country use drugs the least. Metropolis and L.A.–Mex, where by far the most ghetto-dwellers are found, are right on the national average, confirming our observation that ghetto drug use is as limited as it is deadly. There are many people living in our ghettos who don't use drugs, but we seem to hear about only the ones who do.

The drug addicts among our respondents (about 2.9 percent) confessed that they feel terribly depressed about their lives.

We also turned up a number of drug dealers in our interviews and tests.

Profile of a drug dealer:

- The great majority of drug dealers think of themselves as ethical people.
- They, more than others among us, believe that the moral climate has gotten worse in the last thirty years.
- They are more likely to think that their children's schools are dangerous places, and much more likely to think that children learn more bad than good in school.

★ **DRUGS: THOSE MOST LIKELY TO USE**

Four in ten Americans have tried drugs, but the rate varies considerably among different parts of our population:

Group	Percentage Who Have Ever Used Drugs
Men	47%
Women	35
Homosexuals/bisexuals	50
Heterosexuals	43
Whites	42
Blacks	35
Ages 18–24	55
Ages 25–44	49
Ages 45–64	22
Ages 65 and older	3
Liberals	53
Conservatives	30
Single	52
Divorced	50
Married	34
Income less than $10,000	48
Income more than $45,000	38

- Drug dealers have a soft spot for animals. More than the rest of us, they think that animals have rights like people do, that people who wear fur coats are immoral, and that anyone who harms an animal should get a stiff prison sentence.
- Two in five drug dealers have been to church in the last three months.

Which is a good segue. This is our time to talk about God.

A COMPLETE LOSS OF FREEDOM

Novelist William Burroughs attributed much of the sprawling and chaotic structure of his novels to his days as an addict. As a junkie himself, Burroughs understood what *control* and *manipulation* mean. When a junkie wakes up, he has only one choice in the world: to go and get more junk. Burroughs was so affected by this horrifying experience that he didn't want to inflict control or manipulation on his readers—which was one important reason behind the non-structure of his writing.

BY REGION: DRUGS IN AMERICA

(For a map of America's regions, see Part I.)

EVER USED DRUGS (National Average: 41%)

Region	Percentage Who Have Ever Used Drugs	Region	Percentage Who Have Ever Used Drugs
Pac Rim	58%	New South	39%
New England	52	Rust Belt	39
Granary	45	Marlboro Country	35
Metropolis	41	Old Dixie	32
L.A.–Mex	41		

IX

GOD AND OTHER HEROES

29

Religion: Who Really Believes in God Today?

What is going on in congregations, parishes, and synagogues across America? The news is good—and bad.

God is alive and very well. But right now in America, fewer people are listening to what God has to say than ever before.

Ninety percent of the people we questioned said that they truly believe in God.

It would be the logical conclusion then to think that God is a meaningful factor in today's America. But we reached a different conclusion when we dug deeper with our questions.

In every single region of the country, when we asked how people make up their minds on issues of right and wrong, we found that they simply do not turn to God or religion to help them decide about the seminal or moral issues of the day.

For most people, religion plays virtually no role in shaping their opinions on a long list of important public questions. This is true even for questions that seem closely related to religion: birth control, abortion, even teaching Creationism and the role of women in the clergy.

On not one of those questions did a majority of people seek the guidance of religion in finding answers. Most people do not even know their church's position on the important issues.

That, perhaps, is the true measure of Americans' indifference to the teachings of organized religion: We don't follow what our church says because we're not interested enough to find out what it's saying.

THE REAL ROLE OF RELIGION TODAY

As we enter the 1990s, only one American in five ever consult a minister, a priest, or a rabbi on everyday issues.

Half of us haven't been to a religious service for a minimum of three months. One in three haven't been to a religious service for more than a year.

More than half of us (58 percent) went to services regularly while growing up, but less than half of those (27 percent) do so today.

Only one in ten of us believe in all of the Ten Commandments. Forty percent of us believe in five or fewer Commandments.

★	**RELIGION: HOW IMPORTANT IS IT?**		
	Issue	*Percentage of People Whose Religion Had No Role in Shaping Their Position*	*Percentage of People Not Certain of Their Church's Position*
★	School busing	70%	66%
	Flag burning	66	61
	The death penalty	64	57
	Book banning	64	62
	Communism	64	60
	Affirmative action	61	69
★	Birth control	58	46
	Abortion	56	52
	Homosexuality	55	52
	Teaching Creationism in schools	55	52
	Pornography	54	41
	Premarital sex	53	43
	Anti-Semitism	53	56
★	Women in the clergy	52	47
	Racism	48	43
	Prayer in schools	44	35
	Divorce	43	37
	Right to die	43	57

We have established ourselves as the authority on morality. We now choose which Commandments to believe and which ones not to believe. Clearly, the God of the 1990s in America is a distant and pale reflection of the God of our forefathers. This is not the "jealous God" of the Old Testament—six in seven people think that it is okay not to believe in God. Rather, Americans seem to use God to refer to a general principle of good in life—or, sometimes, He (or She) is the creator who set off the Big Bang but doesn't intervene in human affairs.

For most Americans, God is not to be feared or, for that matter, loved.

WHO IS RELIGIOUS IN AMERICA?

There are those who do call themselves truly religious, and some people may be surprised at the demographics.

Ninety-nine percent are under the age of 65.

One in four is a college graduate, and two in three have had some college.

They are more often women. And that fact supports our findings that in this country, women are more moral than men, and religious people are more moral than the national average.

RELIGIOUS PEOPLE ARE MORE MORAL

How does the growing number of nonreligious Americans compare to those who still hold to traditional beliefs? Can a judgment be made about who's more moral?

People describing themselves as "very religious" (14 percent) definitely make better citizens. In the self-portraits they painted for us, the very religious scored much higher than did other people on moral questions that most of us would accept as defining citizenship in a civilized society.

Religious people are far less likely to "have a price." The nonreligious were those 17 percent who defined themselves as being "not religious at all."

WHAT WOULD YOU DO FOR $10 MILLION?		
Would You . . .	Percentage of Religious People Who Agree	Percentage of Nonreligious People Who Agree
Abandon your parents?	17%	37%
Leave your spouse?	11	26
Become a prostitute for a week?	16	38

Religious Americans are more willing to die for what they believe. They're less prone to do something that they know is immoral because others are doing it. They are much more sure of their own moral worth. Three times as many among the religious described themselves as "very good" people.

They are also more at peace with themselves. Religious people are more likely to say they are satisfied with their lives (50 percent vs. 36 percent).

Religious people are much less likely to have used drugs (27 percent vs. 58 percent).

They are more truthful.

They are more committed to the family.

They make better workers, and they are less prone to petty crime.

The religious are also less likely (9 percent vs. 21 percent) to carry weapons.

SIN, AMERICAN STYLE

If religion doesn't give us satisfactory answers, does that mean we believe that there are no rules of morality—that anything goes?

Not entirely.

Americans still have a lively sense of what sin means. And if there is one ideal that underlies our definition of sin, it is the oldest, most universal principle of them all—the Golden Rule. Sin, as most of us see it today, is doing unto others what we don't want done unto ourselves.

GOOD PEOPLE

- Jewish people (41 percent) are the most likely to describe themselves as very good vs. 30 percent of Catholics and 27 percent of Protestants.
- Blacks (34 percent) are more likely to describe themselves as very good than are whites (28 percent).
- The elderly, those aged 65 and over (35 percent), more than 18- to 24-year-olds (25 percent).
- College-educated (35 percent) more than less-educated people (26 percent).
- Homosexuals and bisexuals (30 percent) more than heterosexuals (27 percent).
- Conservatives (33 percent) more than liberals (27 percent).

★ | **BY REGION: WHERE BELIEVERS LIVE**

(For a map of America's regions, see Part I.)

BELIEVE IN GOD (National Average: 90%)

Region	Percentage Who Believe	Region	Percentage Who Believe
Old Dixie	96%	New South	90%
Granary	92	Metropolis	87
L.A.–Mex	91	Marlboro Country	82
Rust Belt	91	Pac Rim	81
New England	90		

Fewer than two people in five believe that sin is "going against God's will" or "going against the Bible" or "violating the Ten Commandments." For the rest of us, sin is defined by our own consciences. We define what is sinful and what isn't.

The Worst Sin I've Ever Committed

Here are examples of what Americans we interviewed remember as the worst sins in their lives:

- "Killed other humans in war."—a post office clerk from the West Coast, forties, Baptist, not a churchgoer.
- "Got into a fistfight with my father. I knocked my father down twice."—a truck driver from Old Dixie.
- "I shot two people once and almost killed them."—a man in his thirties from Old Dixie.
- "Hit my mother."—a single man in his late twenties.
- "Allowed former spouse to physically abuse me without seeking help."—an Hispanic secretary in his early twenties.
- "I once convinced a rich person to invest money in my company and we used it for living."—a real estate agent from the Southwest.
- "Stealing over $500 worth of material from the hospital that I didn't really need."—a registered nurse from the Midwest.
- "Stealing from my uncle, and I am very sorry."—a bank teller from the Northeast.
- "Selling drugs to high-school kids."—a single man from New England, in his early twenties.
- "Being jealous of my next-door neighbor's new car."—a housewife, in her early fifties, churchgoing Catholic.

- "Playing sexually with little girls."—a single man in his late thirties.
- "Having a child out of wedlock."—a sixty-five-year-old woman from the New South.
- "The most serious sin I have committed is not being able to quit drinking and writing bad checks."—a single man, in his late thirties, Lutheran.
- "I had an abortion when I was a very young girl."—a thirty-year-old woman, now divorced and unemployed.
- "Five abortions."—a woman in her late thirties, churchgoer from the South.
- "Stealing and, though not controllable by me, sex with my brothers."—a saleswoman, single, Jewish, attends services regularly.
- "Tried to commit the ultimate sin, suicide."—a disk jockey from the Midwest, single man, Catholic, doesn't attend church regularly.
- "Attempted suicide."—a divorced man in his thirties from New England, Baptist, not a churchgoer.
- "Euthanasia. I helped my sister to die."—a secretary from the Northeast, in her forties, graduated from parochial school, attends church irregularly.
- "Being born."—a retired man from the Northwest, nonreligious.

DO AMERICANS STILL BELIEVE IN HELL?

An afterlife in hell is not something very many Americans honestly fear. Most Americans (82 percent) profess to believe in an afterlife that includes both heaven and hell (55 percent of us believe in the existence of Satan). We are confident, however, that our future prospects are bright. Almost half of us (46 percent) expect to spend eternity in heaven vs. only 4 percent who see their future in hell.

In this respect, we have not lost the optimism for which we are famous.

OTHER POWERS

In addition to God in his heaven and Satan in his hell, these are beliefs that some of us hold:

- Forty-five percent of all Americans believe that ghosts exist.
- Almost one in three (31 percent) believe that some people have magical powers.
- About one-fourth of us believe in witchcraft (28 percent), black magic (24 percent), and voodoo (20 percent).

• And as many as one in twenty Americans have actually participated in some ritual of satanism or witchcraft!

PROTESTANTS, CATHOLICS, OR JEWS: WHO'S MORE RELIGIOUS?

Statement	*Percentage Who Agree*		
	Protestants	*Catholics*	*Jews*
Believe in God	97%	98%	87%
If believe:			
Very sure of God's existence	73	65	27
Believe God created the universe	91	91	56
Believe there is a Hell	94	89	44
Believe there is a Heaven	94	89	53
Not at all religious	7	6	30
Went to church/synagogue often when growing up	67	78	31
Go to church/synagogue often now	34	41	12
Less than 20 percent of life influenced by religious beliefs	13	15	51
Church/synagogue had no influence on moral development	17	19	30

★ **SIN: AS AMERICANS HONESTLY SEE IT**

Americans define "sin" as follows:

Definition	*Percentage Who Agree*
Going against God's will	17%
Any immoral act	15
Willful wrongdoing	13
Harm to self/others	13
Going against one's own beliefs	13
Violating the Ten Commandments	11

AMERICA'S SINS

What are the serious sins people have actually committed? Here's what people confessed in our interviews:

Activity	Percentage Who Admit to Activity
Adultery	24%
Stealing	21
Lying/cheating	15
Disobeying/hurting parent or other relative	10
Premarital sex	8
Slander	6
Disobeying a religious law	4
Greed	4
Having an abortion	2
Attempting/committing murder	2

30

Who Are Our Real American Heroes?

The majority of us (70 percent) believe that America has no living heroes today. About the same number say that our children have no meaningful role models.

More than most of us, people in Old Dixie and in New England still believe in heroes, but even there, less than half are now believers. In the Rust Belt, it's only one in five.

The whole idea of heroes has gotten fuzzy for us. Sometimes it degenerates into TV celebrity. The late historian Barbara Tuchman recalled attending a conference on heroes, held on Superman's fiftieth birthday. She commented:

"It was quite weird, what they considered a hero. The real hero of the discussion was the little girl who'd fallen down a well. She didn't do anything to make herself a hero—she was just in the news. Other heroes discussed were Elvis Presley and somebody whom I had never heard of, the Mayflower Madam."

Nor do we have people in public life we can look up to. Only one-third of us think that the President has any right to tell us what's right or wrong, and far fewer would accept his advice without question.

★ | **AMERICA IN THE POST-HEROIC AGE: WHAT IT ALL MEANS**

In the late 1930s and the 1940s, Joe DiMaggio represented an American ideal. He was the man of deeds rather than of words, whose quiet leadership made him the embodiment of the American hero. Indeed, Ernest Hemingway had DiMaggio in mind when he defined heroism as "grace under pressure." In *The Old Man and the Sea*, the old man cites Joe DiMaggio as proof that heroes really do exist and that man contains within him an unconquerable heroic spark.

It is easy to identify other American heroes from the past: Charles Lindbergh, "the Lone Eagle"; Babe Ruth, "the Sultan of Swat"; Joe Louis, "the Brown Bomber," who demolished Adolf Hitler's claims of Aryan racial superiority by flattening the German "Superman," Max Schmeling. In the movies, John Wayne specialized in playing American heroes.

Seventy percent of Americans now say that America has no more heroes.

Why are there no heroes today? There are no heroes because we have ceased to believe in anything strongly enough to be impressed by its attainment.

- Who really cares how many millions of dollars our athletes will earn?
- Who really cares how many comic-strip villains will get mutilated and massacred by our movie heroes?
- Michael Milken and his $600 million a year salary is to Horatio Alger as today's Madonna is to the historical Madonna—a parody.

An anecdote told by a university president makes the point about our loss of belief in our leaders: In the fall of 1987, he was teaching a Sunday school class for adults that included bankers, business executives, and university professors. He asked them a question based on a then-recent event: "We hear on the news that an Iranian ship has been sunk in the Persian Gulf. The Iranian government says that it was sunk by American

★ | **BY REGION: WHO BELIEVES IN AMERICAN HEROES**

(For a map of America's regions, see Part I.)

BELIEVE THAT AMERICA STILL HAS HEROES (National Average: 30%)

Region	Percentage Who Agree	Region	Percentage Who Agree
Old Dixie	43%	Marlboro Country	31%
New England	42	Metropolis	31
Pac Rim	39	L.A.–Mex	29
Granary	34	Rust Belt	20
New South	31		

torpedoes. The U.S. government says that the ship hit Iranian mines. Whom do you believe?"

The class was silent. No one answered. Everyone wanted more information before deciding what they thought had happened.

Not one person in that class trusted their own government to tell the truth.

They had as much trust in the government of Iran.

★ | **MORAL AUTHORITIES: SOURCES THAT WE WILL ALLOW TO TELL US WHAT IS RIGHT AND WRONG**

Source	Percentage of People Who Say That Source Has Some Right to Tell Them What's Right or Wrong	Percentage of People Who Accept Source's Moral Advice Without Question
Spouse/lover	77%	55%
Parent	71	46
Grandparent	58	37
Best friend	57	37
Bible	52	37
Religion	52	34
Personal doctor	51	37
Child	50	31
Local police	50	33
Church/synagogue	44	25
Government	42	25
Personal lawyer	43	29
U.S. Supreme Court	42	25
Uncle/aunt	42	25
Schoolteacher	39	23
Adult friend	39	22
College professor	37	20
Boss	36	23
President of the United States	32	19
Book	28	11
Co-worker	24	12
Local politician	22	6
TV minister	21	7
The press	21	6
Famous athlete	21	7
Neighbor	19	8
TV personality	19	7
Fictional TV character	19	5
Movie star	19	6

IF NOT GOD, HEROES, OR OUR INSTITUTIONS, THEN WHOM DO WE TRUST?

To whom, or to which institution do most of us turn for moral and ethical advice? When we do turn to someone for help in the 1990s, who is it?

Our church?

Our government? Our schools?

Our parents?

There *is* a clear and overwhelming winner: our spouse or lover.

Everyone else—the traditional authorities—ranks far behind the intimate circle at the top.

Only about one in three Americans accept without question the moral guidance of religion, its practitioners, or its scriptures.

Political figures fare worse.

The Supreme Court commands the allegiance of one in four.

The President is well behind the nine Justices with 19 percent.

Local politicians are way down at 6 percent.

Educators fare no better. Schoolteachers and college professors are considered moral authorities by 23 percent and 20 percent, respectively—although both are among the occupations that Americans most respect.

The saddest showing is by the American press. This institution, much more esteemed a decade and a half ago, when reporters were uncovering the Watergate scandals, has failed terribly in the opinion of most people.

As moral authorities in their lives, Americans rated the press at 6 percent. That's on a par with movie stars, and 1 percent below famous athletes and television personalities.

It is only 1 percent better than fictional television characters.

X

AMERICA AND THE WORLD: WHERE WE ARE NOW AND WHERE WE'RE GOING

31

What Do Americans Really Think About America Right Now?

As a people, Americans show a remarkable ability to distinguish between the country they love and the massive faults they find with it.

Americans believe that our country has become a colder, greedier, meaner, more selfish, and less caring place—yet, for all of its faults, we still love it.

Americans are definitely patriotic—almost unanimously.

Americans' confidence in our major institutions has sunk to an all-time low—but our love for our country is virtually unshaken. The only area where we found such selflessness was when we talked to people about this country.

We are deeply patriotic as a people. Almost all Americans (91 percent) are patriotic and, three to one, we believe that this country needs more rather than less patriotism. Despite all of our criticisms, practically everyone (95 percent) has a deep-down favorable opinion of America.

Indeed, in many ways, we still rate ourselves first. And the great majority of us (81 percent) believe that, first or not, America has a special role to play in the world.

★ | **STILL NUMBER ONE**

Most Americans still rank their country first in these ways:

Aspect	Percentage Who Agree
Democracy	79%
Standard of living	68
World leadership	65
Moral leadership	65
Military strength	63
National pride	60

1973 VS. THE 1990s

What kinds of things upset Americans? How does today compare to earlier days? For argument's sake, let's pick some bad times for our comparison. The year 1973 was a terrible time for American institutions. The Vietnam war, with all of its lessons about our government's ability to lie, was nearing its humiliating end. Driven by high oil prices, the economy was running on double-digit inflation. Forecasters were talking portentously about the disastrous German inflation of the 1920s.

The Executive Branch was in chaos in 1973. The Watergate scandal was unfolding. America was enduring the most compromised Administration in memory, one in which both the President, Richard Nixon, and the Vice-President, Spiro Agnew, were forced to resign.

It was a time when Americans heard their highest elected official announce, "I am not a crook."

You might think that 1973 had to be rock-bottom for us—with no place to go but up.

And yet, America's confidence in the Executive Branch of government has fallen since Richard Nixon left the White House.

America's confidence in our military has fallen since the time of Vietnam.

What's going on appears much deeper than fallout from a government scandal or a lost war.

Since 1973, all of our major institutions have lost ground in our esteem. In fact, many of our institutions have lost more support than have the government and the military.

A KINDER, GENTLER NATION?		
	Which moral attributes are Americans more likely to embody today than in the past?	
Attribute	Percentage of People Who Say that They Are More Likely	Percentage of People Who Say that They Are Less Likely
Materialistic	60%	24%
Greedy	60	21
Selfish	59	15
Criminal	52	21
Phony	48	20
Mean	45	19
Devious	44	21
	Which moral attributes are Americans less likely to embody today than in the past?	
Attribute	Percentage of People Who Say that They Are Less Likely	Percentage of People Who Say that They Are More Likely
Neighborly	62%	18%
Civic-minded	58	19
Patriotic	56	21
Volunteeristic	56	19
Religious	56	13
Honest	54	17
Moral	54	14
Hard-working	53	18
Compassionate	50	15
Charitable	49	20

IT'S WORSE THAN YOU THOUGHT

The year 2000 will find America no longer number one in the world and its domestic sores still running out of control. That's the pessimistic view of most Americans we talked to.

Most Americans now believe that economic power matters more than military power. And half of us believe that we're no longer in first place economically. Far fewer (only 18 percent) think that we'll be first at the turn of the millennium.

According to 52 percent of all Americans, the new economic number one will be Japan. (More about that in Chapter 32.)

★ | **AMERICA'S CLEAR VOTE OF NO-CONFIDENCE**

Here is how the American people's confidence in their institutions has dropped since the mid-1970s:

Institution	Percentage of People Who Had a Great Deal of Confidence		Percentage of Change
	1973	1989	
Executive Branch of federal government	29%	20%	−31%
U.S. Congress	23	17	−26

Institution	Percentage of People Who Had a Great Deal of Confidence		Percentage of Change
	1974	1989	
Organized religion	49%	22%	−55%
Education	49	30	−39
U.S. military	40	32	−20
Major companies	31	24	−23
The press	26	17	−35
Television	23	14	−39
Organized labor	18	9	−50

Institution	Percentage of People Who Had a Great Deal of Confidence		Percentage of Change
	1977	1989	
American banks and other financial institutions	42%	19%	−55%

And what's going on at home? Everyone agrees that we're in deep trouble. What do they say?

1. The President can't do the job. Only 19 percent of us believe George Bush's claim that he will balance the budget by 1993. Even fewer (12 percent) believe that his educational goals will be achieved by the year 2000. More than half (54 percent) believe that Bush will not significantly improve the environment. Most of us (71 percent) emphatically do not believe that America will be a "kinder, gentler nation" when Mr. Bush leaves office.

2. The rich will continue to get richer and the poor poorer (77 percent)

3. The crime rate (official and otherwise) will increase (72 percent)

4. In the year 2000, there will be more violence on our streets (71 percent)

5. Homelessness will increase (62 percent)

6. AIDS will become epidemic in the general population (69 percent) with no cure in our lifetime (60 percent)

7. Drug and alcohol problems will get worse (58 percent)

8. Pollution will increase (62 percent) to the point that life on earth will become unbearable (43 percent)

Don't expect our children to fix America either. Poverty will outlast their lifetime, in the view of most Americans, and so will racism.

Have you noticed that most books and movies about the future portray a world you wouldn't want to live in? More than half of the people we talked to honestly believe that the twenty-first century will be dirtier, harsher, harder, grimier, and gloomier than the world of today.

But not our own futures. That's another story completely.

IT'S BETTER THAN YOU DREAMED

There is a funny Randy Newman song called "My Life Is Good." It's about a Los Angeles couple whose marriage is on the ropes, whose kids are having trouble in school. Oblivious to any of that, the chorus keeps proclaiming, "My life is good! My life is good!"

Like a canoer paddling upstream, most Americans believe that they can go against the current while their country is being swept down the rivers of time.

A majority of Americans see a radically different picture when they look into the future of their country, and their own future.

They believe that for America, things are going to get worse. But for themselves, life is going to get better.

Only one in four of us think that America will be better off a year from now. But the majority believe that we ourselves will be better off—that what happens to America won't happen to us.

Maybe it's all part of our increasing alienation from what happens to other people. (Statistically, this egomaniacal alienation is greatest among the members of the baby bust generation, those eighteen- to twenty-four-year-olds.) We believe that our personal future is not bound up in the fate of our nation. We are islands. We don't really belong to any larger unit.

LIKE PARENT, LIKE CHILD?

Some Americans are more indifferent than others, and the most indifferent are those in the baby bust generation. A 1990 study by the Times Mirror Center was titled "The Age of Indifference." Its subject was "young Americans and how they view the news."

The report's authors concluded: "Young Americans . . . know less and care less about the news than any other generation of Americans in the past 50 years."

In those past decades, Americans aged eighteen to twenty-nine could identify names in the news about as well as their elders could: in the 1940s, Henry Wallace; in the 1950s, Chiang Kai-shek; in the 1960s, Charles de Gaulle; in the 1970s, John Lindsay.

But in recent years, they scored as much as 17 percent below older generations in identifying these names: William Bennett, Thomas Foley, Corazon Aquino, and Vaclav Havel.

The reason is obvious: They don't follow the news, even on TV.

From 1965 to 1990, the percentage of the young who had read a newspaper the day before dropped from 67 to 30. Even the number who had watched TV news was down from 52 percent to 41 percent. Radio, now a principal source of news for those under the age of thirty, was also down. Older people also followed the news less, but the drop wasn't as great as it was among the young.

Some young people try to explain. A twenty-two-year-old woman said, "I don't think many people in my age group are very concerned. They're only concerned about issues that affect them. When the drinking age went up, quite a few people were upset."

A twenty-four-year-old woman said, "I try to avoid all the controversy. It just doesn't interest me at this point in my life. I'd rather be outside doing something, taking a walk."

The young also vote less. The political apathy that characterizes the country is most pronounced among its youth.

Americans aged eighteen to twenty-four are now the only age group in which less than half of those eligible to vote do so.

While the voter turnout for the population as a whole fell from 63 percent of those eligible (in 1972) to 57 percent (in 1988), for the young, it fell more than twice as far. Only among people aged sixty-five and older did voter turnout increase.

What comes after the Age of Indifference—if that indeed is what today's young adults have to offer the country?

MODERN KIDS SAY THE DARNDEST THINGS

To sample the next generation, we talked to a couple of groups of sixth-grade boys and girls. We asked them what they believe in.

The world that American kids know is the world that they see on their TV sets. Period. The Tube is overwhelmingly our children's primary source of information, culture, and morality.

Asked where they got their information on AIDS, they all said, "TV"— every single child in these groups.

Almost unanimously, they do their homework with the TV on because, as one girl said, if it were quiet, "you'd be going berserk."

Like their parents, the young are very short on heroes. The only heroes these children could name from public life were from a time they could only know second-hand: John Kennedy, Abraham Lincoln, Martin Luther King, Helen Keller.

They found no heroes among the living.

A question about politicians brought a chorus of, "They lie." The government was characterized as "cheaters and liars."

Also, like their parents' generation, they are highly materialistic. Asked for their one wish, nearly every boy chose money. The dreams of our children? "Five million dollars and two days at the mall."

Asked about career goals, none chose the helping occupations that our respondents rated highest in moral value.

Among the girls were two future doctors, an actress, two dancers, a writer, and an environmentalist.

Here are some of the things twelve-year-olds told us:

How will the future be for America?

BOYS: "In a word, *worse*."
GIRLS: "It's going down . . . pollution and drugs. . . . We're ruining the ozone layer. We're getting the greenhouse effect. . . . Starvation: the kids in Romania and Africa . . . nuclear wars . . . unless we do something now. But they won't let us."

Which country will be the best by the time you grow up?

BOYS: "Japan . . . Japan. . . . They're growing faster in technology. Japanese work harder than Americans."
GIRLS: "Japanese . . . because they stick to school. They don't have a summer break like we do. They go to school seven or eight hours a day, seven days a week . . . and we'll be the people starving in the future."

What's so different about your lives compared to your parents' lives?

GIRLS: "We have more technology. There's more things to do. You know, they always say that when they were little, there was hop-scotch and jump-rope and all that stuff you play outside . . . we have Nintendo. . . . Yeah, we're always glued in front of the TV."

32

★   ★   ★   ★   ★

Japan vs. America

Considering our past, considering how suddenly it all happened, Americans are taking our fall from grace surprisingly well.

Yesterday we outperformed them.

Today they outperform us. They do it in the marketplace. They even outperform us in that one-time holy of holies, Harvard University.

"They," of course, are the Japanese—other Asians too, but Japanese nationals most of all.

Right now, a majority of Americans (58 percent) genuinely believe that Japan has taken this country's place as the world's leading economic power.

Three-fourths of us also believe that Japan's success in the world market is a violent threat to the United States. That helps to explain why Americans are almost as ready to put someone to death for selling trade secrets to Japan as they are for selling military secrets to the Soviet Union.

In our interviews, the response was a mixed one, however. There was resentment: We blame the Japanese for competing unfairly (64 percent of our respondents said that).

But there was also self-accusation: We blame ourselves for not measuring up to this latest world challenge.

More than half of us (53 percent) believe that American products don't sell in Japan because they're not good enough. Only 38 percent blame Japan's trade practices. Almost half of us (47 percent) believe that Americans are blaming Japan for our own economic problems.

Japan-bashing is a popular phrase. But what does it really mean? We hear it from politicians doing what they do best: attacking an enemy who doesn't vote in their district or give money to most of their campaigns.

★ "JAP-BASHING"

Americans are responding to the emergence of Japan as an economic power and to its apparent competitive edge over the United States with anger, hostility, and veiled (and not so veiled) threats of retaliation:

- 73 percent believe that Japan should be made to pay for its defense costs.
- 63 percent believe that Japan practices an unfair trade policy with the United States.
- 61 percent think that we should restrict the sale of Japanese products in this country.
- 57 percent believe that Japanese ownership of American manufacturing plants represents a threat to our economic independence.
- More Americans think that trade with Japan is bad for the United States (40 percent) rather than good (34 percent).
- 38 percent of Americans believe that we did too much to help rebuild Japan after World War II.
- 34 percent of Americans no longer consider Japan to be a reliable ally.
- 26 percent feel less friendly toward the Japanese as a result of the current trade situation.

BENEATH THE "JAP-BASHING" POSTURE

Under the anger, hostility, and threats of retaliation aimed at the Japanese lies the true heart of the matter: America has lost confidence in itself. We are beginning to believe that the Japanese really must be better than we are.

Do Americans really believe that unfair Japanese trade policies are the reason we can't sell our products in Japan? Not really:

- More than half of Americans (53 percent) believe that U.S. products do not sell in Japan because they are not competitive with Japanese-made products.
- Only 38 percent blame unfair Japanese trade practices.
- More Americans believe that the United States is blaming Japan for its own economic problems (47 percent) than believe that the Japanese are competing unfairly with American companies (35 percent).

We see it in advertising that appeals to nationalist feelings in order to sell goods to people who otherwise might buy Japanese-made products.

Occasionally, an organized group tries to boycott Japanese products. Most Americans (61 percent) actually believe in restricting Japanese sales here. The majority reveal that they would be willing to pay more for U.S.-made equivalents. But these organized efforts, so far, have come to naught.

Although we are resentful, Americans ultimately blame themselves for Japan's industrial superiority. Americans believe that the Japanese are unfair traders, but they don't believe that's why America is losing the trade wars.

Americans believe that the Japanese are superior in every one of the main areas of industrial life: better-skilled and harder-working employees; better-managed companies; better technology; better-educated citizens.

American racial feelings about the Japanese do surface in another way. Here, the issue is foreign ownership of American companies.

In our research, Americans were more concerned about Japanese owners here than they were about the British (who own three times as much of America as the Japanese do). Or those other former World War enemies, the Germans, who actually own about as much of America as the Japanese do.

Most of the people we spoke to (57 percent) believe in their hearts that Japanese ownership of American companies is a threat to the U.S. economy. On the other hand, half of all Americans wouldn't mind working for a Japanese company. Which suggests that there's less wrong with a Yellow Peril if there's a hint of green in it somewhere.

American executives welcome Japan's money, but they too are troubled about Japanese ownership. Some of them attribute that discomfort to what they rather delicately called cultural bias. The blunt fact is that only a fraction of those same executives are uncomfortable about foreign owners who are Europeans. Although more than 40 percent are uncomfortable about the Japanese presence, the figure for Germany is only 6 percent, and for the British 2.5 percent. Indeed, the only owners who make these bosses more uncomfortable than the Japanese do are owners from the Middle East.

Reflecting all of this discomfort, Japanese investment here still makes news, although it's hardly new. More Americans know that the Japanese own Columbia Pictures and Rockefeller Center than know about any other foreign investment in the United States.

Despite the waves it makes, the Japanese stake here is still quite small. Of the 3 million Americans who work for foreign owners, only one in ten has a Japanese boss. Even if, as forecasts tell us, a million Americans will be working for Japanese by the start of the new millennium, that's only 1 percent of the labor force.

Unlike their bonsai and cherry trees, Japanese management methods have not flourished in American soil. American executives working for Japanese companies complained to us that they are left out of decisions made in another country, in another language, by the rules of another culture. There's an irony there that may go unappreciated by many American managers: Their complaints echo those of Europeans working in past decades for American companies' overseas branches.

But Japanese business isn't the only new addition to the U.S. economy; there is also a flourishing of Asians transplanted to these shores.

Asians and Asian-Americans are appearing at the very top of this country's ethnic ladder.

Look at the elite universities that graduate America's future ruling classes: In 1989, Asian-Americans were 28 percent of the freshman class at Berkeley; 18 percent at Stanford; 17 percent at Harvard. They outscore every other group on the mathematics part of the Scholastic Aptitude Test. Asian-Americans dominate in science as well.

At the university level, Asian and Japanese success has aroused relatively mild opposition thus far. The once-excluded Asians are now known as America's "model minority."

★ | **THE SUPERIOR JAPANESE**

Americans overwhelmingly believe the Japanese to be superior in each of the following areas:

Area	United States	Japan
Harder-working workers	19%	78%
Better-managed companies	25	71
Better-skilled workers	36	58
Better-educated citizens	38	58
Better technology	40	56

TOMORROW, THE JAPANESE WORLD

"The future belongs to the Japanese. When I am in France, I am fascinated by the culture, by the decoration, the furniture, the art. But I can't help thinking that a great deal of it belongs to yesterday. Japan, to me, looks like tomorrow—like a view into the twenty-first century."
                                                    —Jay Spectre, interior designer

Can Asian-Americans keep it up academically? Or will later generations fall victim to whatever it is in American society that makes so many
of our children perform below their abilities? Chen Ning Yang, the Nobel
Prize physicist who was raised in China, and who raised his own children
in America, observed:

> "The kids from the Orient are more disciplined. They have a tendency to
> listen to the advice of their parents and their teachers and learn that one
> has to work hard before one can get some enjoyment. Here in America, the
> system is quite different. I noticed, when my children were very little, I
> would say, 'Perhaps you should do this.' They said, 'No, I don't want to do it.'
> 'Why not?' 'Because it's boring.' "

The concept that if something is boring, I don't want to do it, does not
yet exist for most children in Asia. They do not have the idea that they
have to find instant gratification in every venture.

In the America of the 1990s, most of us, especially the young, want to
see something immediately, to see the point. Often that's not the point.

33

Observations and Some Recommendations

Most people lucidly and, sometimes, emotionally told us what troubles them about their lives. Based on what we heard, we drew up a list of what America needs to fix first to be the country its people want it to be. We've also added what we believe are a few solutions.

WHAT AMERICA NEEDS FIXED FIRST AND FIXED FAST

Problem: America has no leaders.

Solution: Business, the major political parties, education, the press, religious groups need to accept right now how incredible poorly they're doing in the eyes of the American people. This is no time to be defensive—the facts are there. We are at a juncture when we either come together or we really fall apart. The American political system must supply clear choices, then more of us have to choose intelligently.

Women, especially, are still not being looked to for leadership. And everything we saw in this study very clearly shows that women are the underutilized hope of this country's future. The time has come for a

Congress dominated by women, for far more women as CEOs, and, yes, for a woman as President of the United States.

Problem: Greed is impoverishing America.

Solution: Make productivity pay. Most Americans want to do that. We could begin by channeling some of the talent and drive that now goes into financial manipulation back into the making of better mousetraps. This can be done without interfering with the energy of the free market.

The American people, acting through government, have always set the rules by which the economic game is played; stagnation has come when government tried to be a player instead of an umpire. Changes in the tax system can make it more profitable to create than to manipulate. Much of the talent that now flows to manipulating the current system will flow to where the rewards are greater: making better goods, providing better services.

We wouldn't be imitating the Japanese. We'd be doing what we do best: rewarding entrepreneurs rather than manipulating the market.

Changes in the rules of the economic game could also encourage long-term employment. We need to give managers motivation to plan for the long pull rather than for the next quarterly statement. America wants a more stable work force, one in which workers care about their firms' future because they plan to spend their own futures there.

A more productive economy produces revenues for other needs as well.

Problem: The state of our education system is a full-scale national crisis right now.

Solution: Make American schools work. A more productive economy will need more skilled workers, and that's only one of the many reasons why America needs far better education than it's getting.

When asked what problems they'd honestly pay "a lot more taxes" or "as much as it takes" to solve, the American people put education first and second (in the form of "eliminating illiteracy").

It can be done. All over America, there are some schools that work beautifully, whether their students are white or black, rich or poor, American or foreign-born. It will take money and intelligence and leadership. We have the first two, but we lack the third.

Finally, education must be made relevant for our young people.

Problem: The earth is sick.

Solution: Make the environment an important unifying cause. This is the issue that is most likely to rouse the interest of those members of the baby boom and the succeeding generation who have dropped out of (or never entered into) the political process.

Saving the earth fits William James's prescription when, in his essay, "The Moral Equivalent of War," he sought to create "without bloodshed" the wartime spirit of unity and service. War today would destroy the earth—saving it seems a sensible alternative. It's also an excellent common enterprise in which to invest the peace dividend that, with luck, could be in store for America in a demilitarized world.

Problem: People today desperately miss the sense of community that comes with belonging to something beyond their immediate, often selfish lives. Throughout the 1980s, we did very little to help one another.

Solution: Americans want to participate in the process by improving our faith in American leaders. Young people don't vote or follow the news, because they don't believe that public events have anything to do with their lives. But America has a long tradition of volunteering. As long ago as the early nineteenth century, a French visitor, Alexis de Tocqueville, commented on the vital role that voluntary organizations played in American life. According to our study, as many as 100 million of us want to help fix America.

It's been thirty years since John Kennedy offered Americans participation in the Peace Corps. They signed up in droves. In recent years, nobody has asked any of us to do anything for anyone except ourselves. Most people we talked to don't understand "a thousand points of light." It is rhetoric and it motivates virtually no one.

Problem: The violence of young males. As we looked over the list of troubles described by our respondents, we were struck by how many of them were connected to young males.

Date rape is almost exclusively committed by young men.

Crime is mostly the doing of young males: If they committed acts of violence at the same rate as the rest of the population, no one would be talking about the crime problem. There wouldn't be any.

Racial violence is mostly the preserve of young men, white and black.

Child abuse, drug addiction, drunk driving: Young men do all of these more than other people do.

Solution: Obviously, this is not a problem to be resolved by a couple of laws and a barrel of money. But leaders who are putting together policies to deal with other questions will gain a dividend if they also ask, "Can what we're doing also be used to reduce violence among young men?" Some form of civilian service for the young—especially young males—is an idea whose time has come.

Other problems that need to be addressed are:

Child abuse: Most people are not aware of the prevalence of child abuse or of the effects it has as abused children grow into adults. Our laws are incredibly fuzzy and unclear in this area, probably because we don't understand what a major and devastating problem child abuse really is in America.

Date rape: People, women especially, want the severity of this problem, the news of it, exposed. They suggest high schools and colleges as proper channels where women can be "gently, sanely encouraged" to report date rape. Once again, relevant education is needed.

Violence: The solution is fairly obvious: Disarm America. Make the penalty for carrying a gun extreme, and then enforce the law. This solution would be unpopular with some, but the vast majority of people would welcome sane, intelligent law-making in the area of gun control.

Poor work performance in American business: Most people are convinced that the number one problem in this area is leadership, specifically, our current crop of executives. As a group, they seem to be motivated by short-term greed; they are not trusted; they do not lead; they are not perceived as moral, ethical people.

Drugs: The American people have more belief in education as a solution here than in the so-called drug war. There is also growing sentiment to legalize some drugs and tax them. Alcohol abuse, meanwhile, remains America's number one drug problem.

The looming Japanese empire: Is the answer more protectionism? Or changing the economic game here to encourage greater productivity? Right now, Americans believe that both protectionism and greater productivity are needed.

34

The Future: 100 Million Volunteers Waiting for the Call

Suppose that the President, especially a Chief Executive in whom people believed, called upon Americans to sacrifice two weeks a year to help solve some of the serious problems in this country. What would actually happen?

We wanted to know, so we asked people if they would give up time to do volunteer work addressed to the country's real problems. A majority of Americans said that they would volunteer up to three weeks right now.

Fifty-eight percent of the American people want to help fix this country, but no one is orchestrating the tremendous energies waiting to be put to work.

Here is what people across the country promised they would do:

- Volunteer work to help prevent child abuse (50 percent)
- Volunteer to help in the area of education and literacy (41 percent)
- Volunteer time to help the environment (29 percent)

Americans have despised taxes and our system of taxation since the Boston Tea Party. But right now, people are so fed up with, and frightened

230

by, our national problems, that 61 percent are willing to pay 10 percent more in taxes.

Almost half of us (46 percent) have at some time refused to buy foreign products (if we thought it would help). Thirty-five percent would be willing to pay as much as 30 percent more for American-made goods.

THE PEOPLE'S NATIONAL AGENDA

Several causes seem to engage the imagination and generosity of the American people right now.

The people we interviewed made it clear to us that they aren't happy with their present apathy. They yearn for the sense of community that they've lost. They're ready for causes that appeal to the best in them, that call on more than narrow self-interest.

★ **THE PEOPLE'S NATIONAL AGENDA**

Based on our research, the American people would pay extra taxes, usually "as much as it takes," to help solve these problems:

★

1. Improving the U.S. education system
2. Fighting illiteracy in this country
3. Putting in safeguards to protect the environment for all of our futures
4. Preventing child abuse in the future and helping child-abuse victims now
5. Doing something meaningful about homelessness
6. Beginning the war on poverty again—in a businesslike manner
7. Fighting the war on drugs

In fact, Americans have always responded better to a crusade than to politics as usual. That's why great politicians turn bread-and-butter politics into crusades. Roosevelt was able to turn the blunt economic issues of the Great Depression into a crusade against fear. The actual policies of FDR's New Deal in its early days mattered far less than the public spirit that he was able to arouse. Kennedy's Peace Corps and space programs did much the same thing for his presidency.

THE TWO E's

In interview after interview, we saw two areas that could be America's unifying causes through the 1990s and on into the next millennium:

Education: a crusade to make America's schools the best, or certainly near the top.

The environment: a crusade to save the earth for our children.

Both stand high on the list of national problems that our respondents are willing to address with their tax money or their time. The figures (almost 40 percent for environment and almost 50 percent for education) show a strong base of grass-roots support, considering that neither has any charismatic voice like FDR's campaigning for it. Such a strong voice could win both causes the enthusiasm of the great majority of Americans.

Both are unifying causes.

Some current causes are not.

Abortion is the issue on which Americans feel most strongly today, but it divides America into two bitterly hostile factions with little apparent way to compromise. Animal rights is also a cause for a minority, but it seems unlikely to capture the allegiance of any majority either.

Neither education nor saving the earth is a new topic, but Americans see both with a new urgency right now.

The First Crusade: Making Our Education System Great

The Asian challenge has crystalized our need for better schools. Even when Americans are asked why the Japanese are beating us on the production line, "better education" is the most frequent answer.

Illustrations of our schools' failure to teach—or our students' failure to learn—boggle the mind:

- American thirteen-year-olds came in dead last in an international math competition; South Koreans ranked first.
- Americans came in last in a nine-country comparison of algebra and calculus scores by the top 5 percent in each country's high-school seniors.
- Average SAT scores declined from 958 in 1967 to 906 twenty years later.
- Two in three high-school juniors can't identify the half-century in which our Civil War took place.
- One in three juniors don't know that Columbus discovered America before 1750.
- More than one-fourth of American high-school students drop out; for blacks, it's 40 percent, and for Hispanics, more than half.
- And so, 27 million American adults are now illiterate.

Americans want their children to be able to read, and count, and find the Persian Gulf on the map.

But they also want schools to teach them values they are not learning at home and elsewhere.

The overwhelming majority of Americans (81 percent) want schools to teach morals to our children. They want their kids to have basic values and a sense of right and wrong.

There are obvious dangers, questions, and problems with this. What values (which means *whose* values) should be taught is one very real question. But most people are saying that it is better to learn values from a textbook than to not learn values at all.

Helping the case for teaching values is a 1990 survey that reveals that students' ethical beliefs are more important than race and class in determining behavior. When 5,000 students in classes from fourth to twelfth grade were asked how they would decide what to do if unsure of right and wrong, they replied:

- "Do what's best for everyone involved" (23 percent).
- "Follow the advice of an authority, such as a parent, teacher, or youth leader" (21 percent).
- "Do what God or Scriptures say is right" (16 percent).

Students who gave any of those answers may make good citizens. They are certainly far *less* likely to lie, steal, or use drugs than are others who said that they would do whatever made them happy (18 percent) or would improve their personal situation (10 percent). They're *more* likely to give to charity, to help the homeless, and to express unpopular opinions.

Better education will take money and something more: our very best people.

Educator Sara Lightfoot talked about the second necessary ingredient: "Tell the country that the way to better schools is to choose better teachers and treat them like chosen people. We need to attract the best people into teaching and then to keep on telling them that they are chosen because they're so good—and to believe that."

Wendy Kopp did it her way. She was still a student at Princeton University when, sitting through a conference on the state of American education, she decided that she would do something herself.

Her answer was a Peace Corps for America's schools, drawn from students at the nation's leading colleges. She named it Teach for America, went out and raised more than $1 million, and recruited 2,500 applicants from which 500 new teachers were to be chosen to teach in rural and inner-city schools, starting in the fall of 1990.

Skeptics pointed out all of the ways the project could fail. To this, Wendy Kopp responded in the spirit of a crusader who doesn't stop to figure the odds: "I don't worry all that much. I really have this attitude that things will all work out. All those little obstacles that people think will stop everything—you can get around anything."

The Second Crusade: The Environment

The votes are also there to save the earth. Americans want to help. They say so in pretty dramatic fashion.

Today, Americans consider acid rain a more dangerous threat than they do the Soviets.

More Americans now identify themselves as environmentalists (39 percent) than as Democrats (31 percent), as conservatives (27 percent), as Republicans (20 percent), or as liberals (9 percent).

Congressional aide Lisa Smith said: "Right now, the environment is about ten times more important to constituents than any other issue."

For occasions like Earth Day, Americans turn out in numbers not seen since the 1960s.

Americans want to see the environment cleaned up, they are willing to pay the bill both in taxes and in local economic impact, and in their own lives they have begun to change their wasteful ways.

The great majority of people we interviewed (85 percent) would try to shut down an illegally polluting plant in their town, even if it meant the loss of jobs—even the jobs of neighbors and family members—even, for better than half of them, their own jobs.

Two-thirds of us are willing to pay $100 a year in added taxes to clean up hazardous wastes.

Four in five want a ban on chemicals that harm the ozone layer, although they know that this would raise the price of goods such as refrigerators and air conditioners.

Most Americans have actually changed their own behavior. Among our respondents, the great majority have recycled cans and newspapers (78 percent), have replaced their gas-guzzler with a more fuel-efficient car (66 percent), and have cut their household use of energy (76 percent). About half have contributed money—and many have given time—to an environmental organization.

And America is willing to do much more. That, indeed, is the final, powerful message we heard on the day when America told the truth.

FIFTY-FOUR
REVELATIONS
FROM
THE DAY AMERICA
TOLD THE TRUTH

---

1. Women are morally superior to men. This is true all across the country—everywhere, in every single region, on every moral issue we tested. Both sexes say so.

Women lie less. Women are more responsible. Women can be trusted more. It is imperative that women be looked to for leadership in America right now in government, in both major political parties, in religion, in education, in business.

2. At this time, America has no moral leadership. Americans believe, across the board, that our current political, religious, and business leaders have failed us. Worse yet is the press. As a moral authority in their lives, Americans rate the press below fictional TV characters.

3. Americans are making up their own rules and laws. Only 13 percent of us believe in all of the Ten Commandments. We choose which laws of God we believe. There is absolutely no moral consensus in this country—as there was in the 1950s and 1960s. There is very little respect for the law or for any law.

4. The official crime statistics in the United States are off by more

than 600 percent. The amount of actual crime in this country is staggering. Sixty percent of us have been victims of a major crime.

5. The 1990s will be marked by very personalized Moral Crusades.
Many of us ache to do the right thing, but we feel that there are no sane
outlets through our institutions. The first Crusade—environmentalism—
is actually happening and this time, we are serious about it. The next
Moral Crusade could be in the area of education. That's where it should
be. Volunteerism is going to happen in a big way.

6. Americans now believe that the Japanese people are superior to us.

7. Lying has become an integral part of the American culture. We lie,
and we don't even think about it. The people we lie to most are those
closest to us.

8. Community, the hometown as we have long cherished it, no longer
exists. There are virtually no hometowns anymore. There is no meaningful sense of community. Most Americans do not participate in any
community action whatsoever.

9. One of our most devastating findings: One in every seven Americans has been sexually abused as a child. This number far exceeds the
statistics published to date. Child abuse is actually creating sociopaths in
this country—at an alarming rate.

10. The ideal of childhood is ending. A tragically high percentage of
American children now lose their virginity before the age of 13.

11. Date rape is a second important, and largely unreported, epidemic. Twenty percent of the women we surveyed report being raped by
their dates.

12. American workers and executives are now willing to sacrifice to
be a part of winning companies. They want to be part of something
bigger and better than themselves.

13. Americans still deeply love America, although they don't expect
it to be number one in the next century, nor even for the rest of this
decade.

14. A men's revolution is brewing—in reaction to the women's revolution.

15. Homosexual fantasies are extremely common in every section of
the United States—one in five of us men and women have homosexual
fantasies.

16. The United States is far and away the most violent industrialized
nation on the earth.

17. We have lost faith in the institution of marriage. A third of married
men and women confessed to us that they've had at least one affair.
Twenty-nine percent aren't really sure that they still love their spouses.

18. There's a breakdown in filial piety—a majority of us will not take care of our parents in their old age.

19. Americans believe in the death penalty. Ninety-five percent of us believe in capital punishment for some crimes. One American in three would actually volunteer to pull the switch for an electric-chair execution.

20. The number one cause of our business decline: unethical behavior by executives.

21. Seventy percent don't believe that America has a single hero right now. George Bush gets some high marks—but mostly because our expectations for the presidency are so low.

22. Eighty percent of us believe that morals and ethics should be taught in our schools. A letdown in moral values is now considered the number one problem facing our country.

23. America's Sodom: It's Beverly Hills, not the South Bronx. The people of Beverly Hills are more likely to have an extra-marital affair and twice as likely to use illegal drugs. The level of child abuse is equal in the two communities.

24. Ninety percent of all Americans believe in God. It is Who that God is that contains the surprises.

25. Religious people are much more moral than nonreligious people.

26. According to over 60 percent of us, Japan will own the next century.

27. American marriage is in crisis. More than half of all Americans genuinely believe that there is no good reason for anyone to get married.

28. America's number one addiction, by far, is alcohol—not drugs.

29. Americans are declaring an end to the cold war. We no longer fear the Russians. What we fear are trade wars—and mostly with the Japanese.

30. Women workers are more ethical. They are less likely to steal, to malinger, to lie to their bosses, to leave early, or to goof off. Women workers are far less likely to drink or use drugs on the job.

31. One-in-three AIDS carriers we talked to have not told their spouses or lovers.

32. The number of sociopaths is increasing at a dizzying rate. The Pac Rim region leads the country in sociopaths.

33. One in seven of us carry a weapon either on our persons or in our vehicles.

34. America's most ethical corporation, according to most people: IBM.

35. The least moral occupations in America include crime bosses, drug dealers, and Congressmen.

36. The most moral occupations include firemen, paramedics, farmers, pharmacists, and grade-school teachers.

37. Hardcore racism is on the decline everywhere, even in the Old Dixie region.

38. Moral ambivalence: Most Americans see the great moral issues of our time in shades of gray rather than as clear-cut moral choices.

39. The death of our authentic selves. Americans are unhappy with who and what they are, wishing to change various aspects of their identities, including their faces, bodies, and accomplishments.

40. There are more Mr. Hydes in our midst than you think. A surprisingly large percentage of us confess to uncontrollable, violent, often sexual thoughts, which we are not always able to control.

41. For a fistful of dollars, we found that Americans would do almost anything: lie, cheat, steal, murder, abandon their families, and change their religion.

42. The battle of the sexes rages on. Men and women continue to report difficulty in understanding each other and hold stereotyped views of how the other sex perceives them.

43. The majority of Americans are malingerers, procrastinators, or substance abusers at work. American workers willingly told us the sad truth about the American work force and why it is becoming ever less competitive.

44. The loss of respect for others' property: Just when the Communists are learning to appreciate the idea of private property, along comes the finding that Americans have little respect for others' property and have a penchant for taking anything that isn't nailed down—from work, at the mall, and on the road.

45. The war against drugs: Another Vietnam? Drugs are not just for junkies anymore. Over 40 percent of adult Americans have tried drugs and almost 20 percent still do. Perhaps that's why Americans don't think that the war against drugs can ever be won.

46. We believe that most of our friends are racists. The company we keep goes a long way toward establishing the kind of person we are. Most Americans, while denying being racists themselves, openly admit that their friends are racist: This is a telling commentary on the state of race relations in America as we enter the 1990s.

47. The new racism: A backlash against affirmative action. Americans no longer support the activist civil rights agenda that characterized 1960s liberalism. They feel that America offers enough opportunities for all ethnic and racial groups to preclude the need for an activist affirmative agenda designed to single out specific groups for special treatment. Indeed, such policies anger and alienate most Americans.

48. The regionalization of moral beliefs: We may be "one nation under God," but there is a tremendous amount of variation in the moral profiles and agendas of Americans in different regions of the country. Vive la différence?—you be the judge.

49. America has no moral leadership. Americans think that our political and moral leaders stink. They feel that they have failed to provide the kind of leadership this country needs and are beginning to despair of ever finding leaders in whom they believe.

50. The United States has become a greedier, meaner, colder, more selfish, and more uncaring place. This is no wild inferential speculation but, rather, the informed consensus of the American people.

51. The end of American hegemony. Americans no longer see America as the cornerstone of the world's economic or political order. It's hard to believe that this defeatist view is held by a nation that no less a moral giant than Abraham Lincoln once termed "the last, best hope of mankind."

52. The great divide: Americans are disengaging their personal futures from our national destiny. Most Americans think that their own futures are going to be fine and dandy. They have become so alienated from the whole that they think they will be individually immune from the fate that they believe will befall the nation as a whole.

53. The failure of our educational system. Unfortunately, a close examination of what Americans think is wrong with our schools puts it all into perspective: Americans' shopping list of education problems sounds more like a prison reform package than a list of educational grievances.

54. The majority of Americans are willing to make sacrifices to make this country stronger and better. We thought that it wouldn't hurt to ask, and they said that they want to help. Now it's up to our leaders to channel this goodwill into positive action—not just feel-good speeches, but a real, hard, direct challenge to Americans to get up off their fannies and do something.

★ | **REVELATION NUMBER FIFTY-FIVE**

In the spirit of truth-telling, this news for the readers of *The National Enquirer*, *The Sun*, and *The Star*.

★ |
Elvis is dead.
Elvis is dead.
Elvis is dead.
Elvis is dead.
Elvis is dead.
—The rock group, Living Colour, from their song, "Elvis Is Dead"

APPENDIX

How We Know What We Know

RESEARCH DESIGN AND METHODOLOGY

Several important steps went into the background, design, implementation, and analysis of this project. The following outline lists the various steps in our research process, the thinking behind each step, and the methodology employed to operationalize each step.

I. Review of secondary data

As originally conceived, this project would rely heavily on existing secondary data on American attitudes and values toward public and private morality. In order to achieve this, we undertook an exhaustive analysis of available secondary data, which included:

- Analyzing data from literally thousands of individual studies conducted over the past thirty years by nearly 100 separate research–gathering entities
- Sifting through over 200,000 potentially useful survey questions
- Conducting an exhaustive review of academic literature and published survey data on issues of private and public morality
- An online search of all newspaper and magazine articles dealing with morality-related issues of the past four years

At the end of all of this research, we were surprised to find that we had little to show for our efforts. Almost no useful data existed that probed beneath the surface of Americans' public positions on the great issues of the day. No significant research had been done on what Americans really believe.

Indeed, with the exception of studies dealing with human sexuality, such as those of Kinsey, Masters and Johnson, Shere Hite, *Cosmopolitan*, and a few academic studies probing into the work ethics of Americans, we found little to use as a starting place for a comprehensive study of Americans' private lives.

Perhaps the greatest shock was that there was not one single comprehensive study anywhere that combined in one cross-referenced database a complete portrait of the public and private spheres of the American psyche. It dawned on us that rather than developing a critical response to "the received wisdom" about what Americans are really like, it was up to us to lay the groundwork for such an endeavor.

II. The cathartic method

The most crucial methodological problem we faced in this study revolved around the issue of how to obtain responses relating to such deeply felt and privately held feelings and convictions. Research techniques used in other studies probing into the private spheres of individuals were inappropriate for our purposes:

- In-depth group interviews: There was just no way that individuals would be open and respond freely in a setting in which others were also present—all we would have obtained was a sampling of what Americans thought that they ought to think and feel and do.
- In-depth one-on-one interviews: While fine for sensitization at the start of the research process, this too would lead to a hesitancy on the part of respondents to be truthful, we believed.
- Telephone interviews: Just as with face-to-face interviews, the problem existed of individuals' inhibitions in telling another person his or her most private thoughts and feelings. It would also have been a logistical nightmare to administer such a long and complex questionnaire over the phone. In addition, we did not feel that respondents talking in their own homes would experience the privacy necessary to truthfully answer the questions.

- A self-administered mail questionnaire: We considered utilizing a self-administered mail questionnaire but considered this method also too fraught with problems.

Undaunted, we developed a technique which, while logistically complex and expensive to execute, allowed us to minimize the various methodological pitfalls described above. We call this methodological approach the cathartic method. We use the term *cathartic* because this method allows the respondent to unburden him- or herself of their closely held secrets at no risk to themselves.

The key to solving the problem lay in guaranteeing absolute privacy and anonymity to the respondent. We wanted to remove all obstacles barring the individual respondent from telling us the truth. We could never completely guarantee that every individual would tell the truth, but we created conditions which minimized the reasons any respondent might have for being less than candid.

- We conducted the interviews in neutral settings guaranteeing privacy and anonymity to the individual respondents.
- Before participating in the survey, respondents were told that the purpose of the study was to probe what Americans honestly believe about a host of topics. A warning label was printed on the covers of the questionnaires which advised respondents:

  "The questions in the questionnaire are highly sensitive and very personal. The questions probe your innermost feelings about some of the most important moral issues of our time—in thought and deed. We don't want surface answers to these questions. We don't want white lies. Please. No white lies. . . . We are looking for total honesty. There are no right or wrong answers. We are concerned only with what you believe . . ."

- Respondents were informed that they would complete the questionnaire in total privacy. They were then able to seal the questionnaires and put them into a locked box so that the field workers would have no way of reading what they had written.
- We utilized the interviewing techniques of the in-depth one-on-one interview to the extent that we asked probing questions to which the respondents were free to respond in an open-ended essay manner and which were often followed by probing follow-up questions aimed at clarifying ambiguous responses.
- The interviews were in the form of a self-administered questionnaire, but unlike the response rate for mailed questionnaires,

the rate for this type of questionnaire could be vastly increased, and we could ensure sample representativeness, reduce respondent selectivity, and guarantee anonymity to the respondent.

A. Questionnaire development

Not having access to the kind of clear baseline data on American morality that we originally anticipated, we decided to develop our own research instrument in such a way that it would allow us to receive feedback from Americans at every step.

- We began by conducting in-depth one-on-one interviews with adult Americans. These interviews gave us our first indication about how deeply we could probe into the private spheres of individuals.
- After developing a rough draft of our questionnaire, we pretested it on a group of twenty respondents. We then debriefed the respondents, asking about problems, questions, or complaints they had with the questionnaire. Armed with this input, we further revised the questionnaire.
- The final questionnaire was then reviewed by two teams of professional survey researchers and social scientists.

B. Questionnaire structure

The questionnaire covered a broad array of moral dimensions. Both closed-ended, multiple-choice-type questions as well as open-ended questions were used. Each question was designed to elicit the maximum amount of information in the shortest period of time. The questionnaire was self-administered.

In order to minimize interview fatigue, individual questions were grouped into interesting and easy-to-digest segments. Then certain question areas were rotated between two different questionnaire versions. Each interview lasted approximately 90 minutes.

Table A.1 lists the various question areas, the number of questions in each area, and the questionnaire rotations.

TABLE A.1

Question Area	Number of Questions	Version 1 (N = 1,000)	Version 2 (N = 1,000)
Addictions	74	X	X
AIDS	20	X	
America's future	54		X
Animal rights	14		X
Authenticity	62	X	
Behind closed doors	116	X	X
Cheating and stealing	53	X	
Community involvement	90		X
Crime and violence	30		X
Death penalty	26		X
Demographics	39	X	X
Divorce	58	X	X
Drug abuse in America	29		X
God and religion	71	X	X
Homelessness	20		X
How good are you, overall?	18	X	X
Impulses	6	X	
Lies	87	X	X
Literacy	23		X
Love and marriage	46	X	X
Moral influencers	79	X	
National defense	9		X
National morality	88		X

Question Area	Number of Questions	Rotation 1 (N = 1,000)	Rotation 2 (N = 1,000)
Occult and supernatural	11	X	
Parents, children, and filial piety	43	X	
Personal definitions of morality	15	X	X
Physical violence	45	X	
Religion	32		X
Rich vs. poor	78		X
Secrets, privacy, trust	55	X	X
Sexual cheating	53	X	X
Suicide	17	X	X
The battle of the sexes	84	X	
The environment	9		X
The moral climate	47		X
The new immigrants	20		X
Work	201	X	X
Total questions	1822		

C. The sample

Our main sample consisted of a randomly drawn sample of 2,000 adult Americans. The survey was administered by a leading international research firm. The survey was conducted in fifty locations, regionally dispersed so as to get high geographic representation of the United States. The geographic composition of the sample is shown in Table A.2.

TABLE A.2

Region of the Country	Percentage of U.S. Population	Percentage of Surveyed Respondents
Middle Atlantic	21.6%	22%
New England	4.9	4
West North Central	5.1	4
East North Central	16.8	18
South Atlantic	15.1	16
East South Central	4.6	4
West South Central	9.1	10
Mountain	4.1	4
Pacific	18.4	18

The margin of error (statistical significance) for the univariate statistics reported in this book and based on the survey, can be inferred from Table A.3.

TABLE A.3

Margin of Error	Confidence Level				
	95%	90%	85%	80%	75%
For N = 1,000					
Univariate data	+3.1%	+2.6%	+2.3%	+2.0%	+1.8%
Male/female	+4.4%	+3.7%	+3.2%	+2.9%	+2.6%
For N = 2,000					
Univariate data	+2.2%	+1.8%	+1.6%	+1.4%	+1.3%
Male/female	+3.1%	+2.6%	+2.3%	+2.0%	+1.8%

D. Quality control

At each step in the research, we made crucial methodological decisions that we felt would make this a more scientifically valid and reliable study. Listed below are the various precautions we took to ensure against the most common pitfalls of empirical research. Because the reader may not have a technical knowledge of just what these pitfalls are, we have decided to provide them and to describe their applicability to this study and the steps we took to minimize them.

W. Edwards Demming, a classical social research methodologist, identified thirteen sources of error in survey research. The method selected for this project was specifically designed to maximize both the reliability and validity of the data obtained by minimizing each of the thirteen potential sources of methodological error.

1. Variability in response

[The same respondent may give different responses to the same question at various points in the questionnaire, rendering the validity of his or her responses questionable.]

This issue was addressed by including failsafe measures into the questionnaire design, such as making sure that respondents who answered questions about being divorced also gave their marital status as divorced in the demographics section, or that respondents' answers about their children corresponded with respondents' reporting having children later in the questionnaire, and so on. Respondents giving inconsistent responses were eliminated from the pool of analyzed data for each particular subsegment of the questionnaire.

2. Differences in forms of interviews

We believe that for the objectives at hand, a self-administered interview, with pre-interview screening for suitability and sampling fit, and post-interview cross-checking of interview completion, was the most suitable form for such a questionnaire as ours. This ensured a representative sample, adequate completion rates, and, at the same time, provided the interview subject with total anonymity in a private and anonymous setting.

3. Bias and variation arising from the interviewer

The self-administered nature of the survey instrument eliminated any possibility of interviewer bias.

4. Bias arising from the agency supporting the research

[That is, the individual may be hesitant to reveal his or her responses to an agency that may use the responses in a manner detrimental to the respondent.]

This source of error does not really apply to this project, because it was made clear to all respondents exactly what the purpose of the research was, as well as the steps that we were taking to ensure their absolute anonymity and the privacy and confidentiality of their responses.

5. Imperfections in the design of the questionnaire

[Lack of clarity in the interview questions, different meanings of the same word to different groups of people, etc.]

We took special steps and went to a great deal of expense to minimize this type of error:

- First, we conducted thirty intensive one-on-one in-depth interviews to probe the depth of response we might be able to expect from respondents, as well as to determine in which subject areas people just wouldn't respond.
- Second, we tested a rough-draft version of the questionnaire on a group of twenty respondents and then debriefed the respondents, probing for any ambiguities or improper or offensive questions that might lead respondents to break off from the questionnaire. In addition, respondents were asked to explain what specific questions meant, thus ensuring that the meaning of the questions was clear and unambiguous.

6. Changes that take place in the sample universe before analysis is completed

This kind of error is much more appropriate for political or attitudinal research, which attempts to take the public's changing attitudinal pulse. The nature of our research, by virtue of the depth and breadth of its scope, is much less likely to suffer from outdating.

7. Bias that arises from nonresponse rates

[Nonresponse may erode the validity of the research sample.]

Because respondents for this survey were prerecruited, with field researchers meeting strictly defined sampling quotas, respondent nonresponse was a nonissue in this research. Almost 100 percent of recruited respondents finished the entire questionnaire, and respondents refusing to be screened were replaced by similar respondents with identical demographic characteristics—this was expensive, but quite effective.

8. Bias arising from late reports

Because this was not a mail survey, this type of bias was not a problem.

9. Bias that arises from an unrepresentative selection of a date for the survey or of the period covered

The questionnaire was administered over a week, so that both weekday and weekend responses could be included. In addition, special care was taken to ensure that interviewing did not overlap any national or religious holidays or other special events of monumental national interest.

10. Bias that arises from an unrepresentative selection of respondents

After accumulating, coding, and processing the questionnaire, the demographic parameters of our sample were compared with the demographic parameters of the desired sample universe and found to be acceptable.

11. Sampling errors

A perusal of the section II.C above will provide the reader with a detailed discussion of the size of our sampling error and an indication of the differences required for statistical significance in various situations.

12. Errors of processing, coding, editing, and tabulating

With the advent of computer technology, these types of errors have been reduced significantly. However, special care was taken to ensure that the data were properly and cleanly coded.

With respect to open-ended responses, all coding was set up and supervised by senior researchers, after having agreed upon beforehand the parameters of the various answer categories, and after having test-coded many sample questionnaires to ensure agreement on how specific responses were to be coded.

13. Errors in interpretation

Again, the elaborate prequestionnaire in-depth interviews and pretesting of a pilot version of the questionnaire allowed us to double-check and make absolutely sure that respondents were saying what we thought they were saying and to double-check this by directly asking respondents what they thought the questions meant.

III. Morality quizzes

Although our major thrust was to design a comprehensive study of Americans' public and private moral domains, we felt that it was useful to develop a series of morality quizzes. The quizzes were designed to allow the reader of this book to compare his or her morality quotient with that of the average American.

For this purpose, we surveyed a second random national sample of 3,577 respondents. They were interviewed via a mail questionnaire, because the nature of the questions was of a decidedly less personal and less sensitive nature. We mailed out 9,083 questionnaires and received 3,577 completed questionnaires (an effective completion rate of 39.4 percent).

Table A.4 lists the various question areas, the number of questions in each area, and the questionnaire rotations.

TABLE A.4

Question	Number of Questions	Version 1 (N = 1,869)	Version 2 (N = 1,708)
Are you true to yourself?	21	X	X
Are you really a good person?	19	X	X
Are you an ethical employee?	23	X	X
Are you an ethical boss?	29	X	
Are you a racist?	36		X
Are you a good American?	14	X	X
What do you believe our future will be like in the next 50 years?	29	X	X

The margin of error (statistical significance) for the test results can be inferred from Table A.5.

TABLE A.5

Margin of Error	Confidence Level				
	95%	90%	85%	80%	75%
For N = 1,869					
Univariate data	+2.3%	+1.9%	+1.7%	+1.5%	+1.3%
Male/female	+3.5%	+2.9%	+2.5%	+2.3%	+2.0%
For N = 1,708					
Univariate data	+2.4%	+2.0%	+1.7%	+1.5%	+1.4%
Male/female	+3.5%	+2.9%	+2.6%	+2.3%	+2.1%

IV. In-depth focus groups

In-depth group interviews were conducted in order to deepen our understanding of the attitudes that men express about women and the attitudes that women express about men. These interviews deepened our understanding of how men and women view each other and assisted in our interpretation of the battle-of-the-sexes data from our main questionnaire.

In-depth group interviews were also held with twelve-year-olds. These interviews probed into the moral universe of preadolescents.

V. Beverly-Hills-vs.-South-Bronx survey

A telephone survey was conducted, using a sample of randomly generated telephone numbers, among residents of Beverly Hills, California, and the "Fort Apache" section of the Bronx in New York. Fort Apache area was defined as the 41st Precinct of the New York City Police Department.

In all, 109 interviews were completed in Beverly Hills and 102 in Fort Apache. Each interview lasted about twenty minutes. The questionnaire was designed as a barometer, based on our master questionnaire. The results from this survey were used to compare and contrast the moral landscape of the two communities in terms of their deeply held values and beliefs.

Notes

INTRODUCTION

Page 3   Statistics for the 1950s and 1990s: Simmons Market Research Bureau; Television Bureau of Advertising; U.S. Department of Commerce; Bureau of the Census, *Historical Statistics of the United States, Colonial Times to 1970*; and *Statistical Abstract of the United States 1990*; U.S. Federal Bureau of Investigation; *World Almanac 1990*.

Page 5   Women At the Top: American Council on Education, *Women University Presidents*, 1990; *Business Month*, April 1990; Congressional Directory, *Women in Congress*, 1989–1990.

Page 7   "Like most men . . .": Bourjaily, Vance: *Confessions of a Spent Youth* (New York: Dial, 1960), p. 3.

PART I

Page 11   Garreau, Joel: *The Nine Nations of America* (Boston: Houghton Mifflin, 1981).

Page 13   How we defined the nine moral regions of America: First step in our analysis was to examine currently existing geo-segmentation frameworks. We looked at regions of the country as defined by the Census Bureau (e.g., Northeast, Middle Atlantic, West, and so on) and also state boundaries as a way of geographic segmentation. However, these boundaries tend to be rigid in nature and not fully reflect regional changes that happen over time. Finally, we chose Areas of Dominant Influence (ADI) as defined by ARBI-TRON, Inc., as our building blocks. It should be noted that ADI boundaries cut across state lines.

The second step in our analysis was to integrate and synthesize all the existing knowledge about demographic, cultural, and geographical regions. We utilized a wide variety of data sources including the Census Bureau, Donnelley Marketing Information Services, Simmons Market Research Bureau, and our own proprietary databases, to develop this new moral landscape of America.

The third step was to develop hypotheses about which areas belong together. In testing these hypotheses, we were looking for similarities within a region and differences across regions. This process of defining, testing, and refining yielded the Nine Moral Regions of America.

PART II

Chapter 1

Page 29   Lies We've Been Told by the Very Best: Richard M. Nixon, quoted in the *Christian Science Monitor*, February 5, 1986; Donald Trump, Gary Hart, Beech-Nut Corporation, quoted in the *Washington Post Magazine*, December 27, 1987; Ronald Reagan, quoted in the *New Republic*, July 31, 1987.

PART III

Chapter 3

Page 39   American Genius at Duplicity?: Gamal Abdel Nasser, quoted in Winokur, Jon: *The Portable Curmudgeon* (New York: New American Library, 1987), p. 17.

Chapter 4

Page 47   The Power of a Lie: Sissela Bok, quoted in Moyers, Bill: *Bill Moyers: A World of Ideas* (New York: Doubleday, 1989), p. 236.

Chapter 5

Page 54   1981 Figures: American Society of Plastic and Reconstructive Surgery.
Page 54   1989 Projections: *U.S. News & World Report*, May 1, 1989.

PART V

Chapter 12

Page 95   A Scarlet Letter in Modern-Day Wisconsin: Jay S. Moynihan, quoted in the *New York Times*, April 30, 1990.
Page 95   Even Birds Do It: the *New York Times*, science section, August 21, 1990.

Chapter 13

Page 100   "I'll tell you . . .": a teacher quoted in the *Los Angeles Times*, September 8, 1988.
Page 101   Figures for Early Sex: *Family Planning Perspectives*, March/April 1987, p. 46.
Page 102   California High School: *Life*, July 1989.
Page 103   Danielle and Cosmetic Sales: *Redbook*, March 1990.
Page 104   "There was a time . . .": the *Los Angeles Times*, September 8, 1988.
Page 104   Dating in the Fourth Grade: the *New York Times*, May 3, 1990.
Page 105   Bret Easton Ellis, *Less Than Zero* (New York: Simon & Schuster, 1985).

PART VI

Chapter 15

Page 119 Robert Louis Stevenson, *Dr. Jekyll and Mr. Hyde* (New York: Bantam, 1982).

Page 120 Violence: The U.S. vs the World: World Health Organization Statistics, 1988; the *New York Times*, June 27, 1990.

Page 120 The Modern Killing Fields: World Health Organization Statistics, 1988.

Page 121 True Confessions: Michael Slackman, "A Gruesome Confession," *Newsday*, July 20, 1989, p. 20.

Page 123 Summer Movie Body Count: the *New York Times*, July 16, 1990.

Page 123 Violent Acts per Hour on Children's TV: Associated Press, January 25, 1990.

Page 123 "Humorous" Violence: *Ibid.*

Page 123 Action for Children's Television: United Press International, June 5, 1990.

Page 124 "The heroes are usually white . . ." Petra Hesse, quoted in *Health*, July/August 1990.

Chapter 17

Page 129 Victims Don't Report: *Chicago Tribune*, March 19, 1989.

Page 129 David Elkind, *Hurried Child: Growing Up Too Fast Too Soon* (Addison-Wesley, 1989).

Page 129 University of Massachusetts Survey of Undergraduates conducted by Professor Michael Shively, 1988.

Page 129 "Who would believe me . . .": quoted in Robin Warshaw, *I Never Called It Rape: The Ms. Report on Recognizing, Fighting, and Surviving Date and Acquaintance Rape* (New York: Harper & Row, 1988), p. 30.

Page 129 "I felt I couldn't go . . .": *Ibid.*, p. 115.

Page 129 "I *felt* raped . . .": *Ibid.*, p. 53.

Page 129 "I never told anyone . . .": *Ibid.*, p. 120.

Page 130 "Both of the guys . . .": *Ibid.*, p. 86.

Chapter 18

Page 131 "People have a tendency . . ." Lee Brown, quoted in the *New York Times*, July 27, 1990.

Page 131 "There is an overall . . .": Joseph R. Borelli, *Ibid.*

Page 133 Suicide Figures: U.S. National Center for Health Statistics, "Vital Statistics of the United States Annual," 1988.

PART VII

Chapter 20

Page 141 Mark Twain, *Pudd'nhead Wilson* (Penguin, 1969).

Chapter 21

Page 147 America and Japan: Akio Morita, quoted in Akio Morita & Shintaro Ishihara: *The Japan that Can Say 'No'* (Kobunsha Kappa-Holmes), p. 41.

Page 148   Ten Very Large Golden Parachutes: *Business Week,* May 7, 1990.

Page 148   "The older hands get depressed . . .": Jere Henshaw, quoted in the *Los Angeles Times*, April 22, 1990.

Page 150   Business Ethics in the News: the *New York Times*, July 27, 1990.

Chapter 22

Page 157   Integrity Testing at Super D Drugstores: the *New York Times*, February 11, 1990.

Page 158   Bosses and Workers: Kevin Phillips, quoted in the *New York Times*, June 17, 1990.

Page 158   High-School Seniors: 1989 Study by Pinnacle Worldwide of 705 business people and 1,093 seniors.

Page 159   What Middle Class Kids Miss: Willard Gaylin, quoted in Bill Moyers, *Op. cit.*, p. 120.

Page 159   The Price of Success: Michael Josephson, quoted in Bill Moyers, *Op. cit.*, p. 15.

PART VII

Chapter 23

Page 165   Figures on income, etc., in Beverly Hills and the South Bronx: U.S. Bureau of Census, and Donnelley Marketing Information Services, 1989.

Chapter 24

Page 170   White Picket Fences: David Lynch, quoted in *People*, July 9, 1990.

Chapter 25

Page 174   "Crime in the U.S.": U.S. Bureau of Crime Statistics, 1988.

Page 175   "Mama Tried": the *New York Times*, April 10, 1990.

PART IX

Chapter 30

Page 207   America in the Post-Heroic Age: What it All Means: Barbara Tuchman, quoted in Bill Moyers, *Op.cit.*, p. 7.

Page 207   Persian Gulf Story: Bill Moyers, *Op. cit.*, p. 239.

PART X

Chapter 31

Page 213   Patriotism Figures: The Times Mirror Center, "The People, The Press, and Politics," March 1989; the *Los Angeles Times*, October 15, 1988; The Gallup Organization, Gallup Poll, April 16, 1989.

Page 214   "I am not a crook": Richard Nixon, to the Associated Press Managing Editors Association at Disneyland, November 17, 1973.

Page 216   America's Clear Vote of No-Confidence: National Opinion Research Center, General Social Survey, 1973, 1974, 1977, 1989.

Page 218 "I don't think many people . . .": the *New York Times*, June 28, 1990.
Page 218 "I try to avoid . . .": *Ibid.*

Chapter 32

Page 222 "Jap-Bashing": The Times Mirror Center, "The People, The Press, and Politics," March 1989; ABC News/*Washington Post*, February 1989; *Time*/Cable News Network, June 1989; CBS News/*New York Times*, February 1989; Associated Press/Media General, July 1989.
Page 222 "Beneath the Jap-Bashing" Posture: Louis Harris & Associates, "Harris Poll," November 14, 1988; Maryland Public TV, "Opinion Research Survey," January 8, 1989.
Page 223 Executives' response to foreign ownership: Conference Board: Chief Executive Opinion, February 1990.
Page 224 Asian-Americans in College: *Washington Post*, March 8, 1990.
Page 224 Tomorrow, the Japanese World: Jay Spectre, quoted in *Insight*, November 3, 1986.
Page 225 "The kids from the Orient . . .": Chen Ning Yang, quoted in Bill Moyers, *Op. cit.*, p. 305.

Chapter 34

Page 232 Figures on school failure: "Mathematics: The Findings," A World of Differences, Educational Testing Service & International Assessment of Educational Progress, 1988; "Second International Mathematics Study" conducted by the International Assessment of Educational Progress, 1982; "National College-Bound Senior," College Entrance Examination Board, 1988; "Class of 2000," *The Futurist*, November–December 1988, pp. 9–15; "Report on Education," Joint Economic Committee, April 18, 1989; Lauro Cavazos, "Restructuring American Education Through Choice," U.S. Secretary of Education, May 19, 1989.
Page 233 Students' ethical beliefs: the *New York Times*, March 17, 1990.
Page 233 "Tell the country . . .": Sara Lightfoot: quoted in Bill Moyers, *Op. cit.*, p. 165.
Page 233 "I don't worry all that much . . .": Wendy Kopp, the *New York Times*, June 20, 1990.
Page 234 How Americans Identify: "Americans identify themselves as Environmentalists," *Research Alert*, January 8, 1988, p. 10.
Page 234 "Right now, the environment . . .": Lisa Smith, quoted in the *New York Times*, July 29, 1990.

Index